CONVERSION-INITIATION AND THE BAPTISM IN THE HOLY SPIRIT

An engaging critique
of James D.G. Dunn's
Baptism in the Holy Spirit

Howard M. Ervin

HENDRICKSON
PUBLISHERS
PEABODY, MASSACHUSETTS 01961-3473

To the memory of
HARRY and FLORENCE ERVIN
Parents whose loving sacrifices
made possible a son's entrance
into the Christian ministry

Reference is made to *Baptism in the Holy Spirit*, by James D. G. Dunn. Copyright © SCM Press Ltd., 1970, published in the U.S.A. by the Westminster Press. Used by permission.

Scripture quotations are from the Revised Standard Version, Copyright © Division of Christian Education of the National Council of Churches in the United States, 1946, 1952, © 1971, 1973. Used by permission.

CONTENTS

iii

Preface

The nature of James D. G. Dunn's book has, in turn, determined the methodology employed in this critique. Since his work is an exegesis of the Greek text of the New Testament, a rebuttal necessitates a close scrutiny of the grammatical, syntactical, and contextual evidence offered in support of his conversion-initiation thesis. Consequently, while there are numerous quotations from the Greek text which are essential to the interpretation, these should not prove to be an insurmountable barrier to the interested layman. Each quotation is accompanied with a translation in English that should make the argumentation intelligible to the reader who does not understand the Greek text.

Responding, as I have, within the context of Dunn's argumentation has determined the scope and content of my response. This has involved a certain amount of repetition as familiar arguments are rehearsed in different contexts. No attempt has been made to present a systematic and comprehensive theological synthesis of the conclusions reached. Rather, I have limited myself to an examination of the inadequacies and errors in the exegesis offered in support of the conversion-initiation thesis. I have simply accepted the gauntlet wherever Dr. Dunn has thrown it down. My rebuttal is, therefore, frequently of the genre "Hoist with his own petard."

It is a wry commentary on the sectarian nature of the debate that some Sacramentalists have seen in Dr. Dunn an ally for their own anti-Pentecostal biases. On the other hand, there are Pentecostals who have taken comfort in his antisacramentalism. Apparently neither side has recognized the true nature of the case. Given the metaphysical presuppositions implicit in the conversion-initiation thesis neither side can really take comfort in his conclusions. Dr. Dunn's perception that Pentecostals and sacramentalists share a common world-view is correct, whether they choose to acknowledge it or not. If his anti-Pentecostalism is right, then so also is his antisacramentalism. On the other hand, if his antisacramental polemic is in error, then so also is his anti-Pentecostalism. It is the conclusion of the following critique that he is wrong on both counts.

The successful completion of this manuscript is due in no small measure to the administration of Oral Roberts University, particularly Dr. James B. Buskirk, Dean of the Graduate School of Theology, for arranging my sabbatical leave for the spring semester of 1982. My sincerest thanks are due to faculty colleagues who have supported this undertaking. I owe a special debt of gratitude to Dr. M. Robert Mansfield whose patience has been inexhaustible in reading and discussing some of the more abstruse questions of Greek grammar and syntax. In addition, Bishop Mack B. Stokes and Dr. J. Michael Miller reviewed the entire manuscript, while a former graduate student, Dr. John G. Schwane, offered a helpful critique of the "Excursus on Acts 4:8, 31; 13:9." This is not to infer, however, that these colleagues share my own theological views. I assume full responsibility for the conclusions expressed herein.

A special word of appreciation is due Mr. Robert W. Graves who read and critiqued the manuscript in an original draft. His comments and shared research have made a significant contribution to the formulation of the views expressed at critical points in the discussion. The accompanying indices are evidence of his interest in, and support of, this project. Appreciation is due also to Mr. Lynn Nichols of the University Office of Public Relations whose editorial expertise is to be found on every page of the completed text. An additional word of appreciation is due also to Hendrickson Publishers, and in particular, Dr. Ben Aker, general editor, for their expertise and interest shown in the preparation of the manuscript for publication. My thanks are extended also to Mrs. Walter S. Pula who painstakingly typed the manuscript. Last, but not least, it is a special joy to acknowledge the constant support and encouragement of my wife, Marta, during the long months of research and writing.

Introduction

James D. G. Dunn characterized his book, *Baptism in the Holy Spirit* as *A Re-examination of the New Testament Teaching on the Gift of the Spirit in relation to Pentecostalism today.* Copyrighted by SCM Press Ltd. in 1970, and published in the United States by Alec R. Allenson Inc., it is one of the monographs in *Studies in Biblical Theology, Second Series.*

As one of the most comprehensive and influential rebuttals of Pentecostalism today, it continues to exert considerable influence upon the theological debate evoked by the widespread emergence of Pentecostal phenomena in both Protestant and Catholic churches. In the opinion of some protagonists I have encountered, it is regarded as the final and definitive word on the subject, an opinion vigorously challenged in the ensuing critique.

Its acceptance may be judged, in part, by the fact that Westminster Press reprinted it in 1977 as a "classic." This latter publisher summarizes its message thus, "What Dr. Dunn uncovers here is the place of the gift of the Spirit in the total complex event of becoming a Christian. His conclusions will help the reader to deepen his own understanding of the sacrament of baptism." Nor is this all, for in Donald Guthrie's, *New Testament Theology*, published by Intervarsity Press, 1981, he refers to Dunn more than to any other author—at least 20 times in his chapter on the Holy Spirit.

At the risk of oversimplification, the crux of the following discussion may be summarized thus. It is a consensus of the classical Pentecostal view that the baptism in the Holy Spirit (Acts 2:4) is *subsequent* to conversion and the new birth. This argues for two clearly distinguishable actions of the Holy Spirit in the life and experience of the believer. Furthermore, it is widely held in Pentecostal circles that the reception of the Pentecostal baptism in the Spirit is evidenced by the phenomenon of speaking in tongues (glossolalia). While not all Pentecostals hold to this doctrine of "initial evidence," the significant role of glossolalia in the experience of Spirit-baptism is widely endorsed.

To this Pentecostal understanding of Spirit-baptism, Professor Dunn offers a theological construct distinguished by the hyphenated title "conversion-initiation." In this conversion-initiation thesis developed by Dr. Dunn, repentance, faith, baptism, *and* the gift of the Holy Spirit represent an indivisible unity without which one is not a Christian. That is to say, one is not a Christian until he has experienced all elements of this conversion-initiation paradigm. It is this schema that provides the basis for his rejection of the Pentecostal understanding of the baptism in the Spirit, *subsequent* to conversion and the new birth, for power-in-mission.

Ancillary to Dunn's anti-Pentecostal posture is an equally unquestionable rejection of all sacramentalism. The rationale for this twin polemic is clearly discernible. However attenuated one's doctrine of baptismal regeneration, or justification, may become, a sacramental realism does, in the nature of the case, argue for a *subsequent* Spirit-baptism. Moreover, after examining the conversion-initiation thesis more closely, another common denominator is discernible in the author's twin polemic. Implicit in his methodology are metaphysical assumptions about the nature of spiritual reality. This question is addressed specifically in the ensuing critique.

Chapter 1

John's Baptism in the Spirit and Fire

The chapter on "The Expectation of John the Baptist"[1] is preparatory to the development of Dunn's conversion-initiation thesis. Its contribution to the author's debate with Pentecostals is summarized thus:

Any idea of a baptism in the Spirit as something which those already in the Kingdom might yet be without is totally excluded. The baptism in the Spirit was not something distinct from and subsequent to entry into the Kingdom; it was only by means of the baptism in the Spirit that one could enter at all.[2]

This contention is open to the following objections. (1) The argument confuses prophetic eschatology and apocalyptic eschatology. John's anticipated baptism in the Spirit and fire belongs to the fulfillment of OT prophetic eschatology. This eschatological time frame is decisively altered by the apocalyptic discourses of Jesus just prior to His crucifixion. (2) In Peter's application of Joel's prophecy (Acts 2:17), the disciples in Jerusalem are already Yahweh's "menservants and maidservants" prior to their baptism in the Spirit on the day of Pentecost.

Of the eschatological baptism in the Spirit and fire (Matt. 3:11; Luke 3:16), it is remarked that:

It was the fiery πνεῦμα in which all must be immersed as it were, and which like a smelting furnace would burn up all impurity. For the unrepentant it would mean total destruction. For the repentant is would mean a refining and purging away of all evil and sin which would result in salvation and qualify to enjoy the blessings of the messianic kingdom.[3]

Partial agreement is possible with at least the first part of this conclusion. It would mean destruction for the unrepentant. John's eschatological baptism in the Spirit and fire, however, has its own distinctive time frame in salvation history. It belongs to the fulfillment of OT prophetic eschatology, an eschatology foreclosed by Jesus' sentence of interdict upon the leaders of the nation—"the kingdom of God will be taken away from you and given to a nation producing fruits of it" (Matt. 21:43).[4] The baptism in fire portended destruction for the unrepentant, and the eschatological discourses in the Synoptics are the messianic pronouncement of judgment upon those who refused to repent and prepare for the advent of the kingdom (cf. Luke 21:20-24).

In His lament over Jerusalem, Jesus bewailed their refusal to repent and concluded, "Behold, your house is forsaken and desolate" (Matt. 23:38). The motif of judgment is intensified in the context by the scathing woes pronounced against the scribes and Pharisees. These woes serve to introduce His lament over Jerusalem. The fall of Jerusalem to the Roman legions in A.D. 70 bears tragic witness to the fiery and bloody "baptism" that closed the age for the unrepentant.

On the other hand, the Pentecostal baptism in the Spirit is set in a different eschatological time frame. Categories appropriate to John's prophetic eschatology—total destruction, refining and purging of sin, the blessings of the messianic kingdom—cannot be extended ambiguously to refer to the Pentecostal baptism in the Spirit for power-in-mission. These categories take on different nuances after Pentecost appropriate to the global mission of the Church. In Pauline terminology, for example, "There is therefore now no condemnation for those who are in Christ Jesus" (Rom. 8:1).

Pentecost belongs to the epoch of apocalytpic eschatology, and its predicates are addressed to the already saved. For instance, the pouring out of the Spirit upon the 120 disciples in Jerusalem on the day of Pentecost did not result in their salvation. Rather as F. F. Bruce has observed, "The effect of the Spirit's outpouring is the prophetic gift exercised in visions and dreams and by word of mouth."[5]

According to the prophecy of Joel, the Spirit is to be poured out "on my menservants and my maidservants" (Acts 2:18). In Peter's application of the prophecy to the Christian community in Jerusalem, they were already Yahweh's "menservants and maidservants" before their baptism in the Spirit. This is a pointed refutation of the claim that "any idea of a baptism in the Spirit which those already in the Kingdom might yet be without is totally excluded."[6] Clearly, this is precisely what Luke would have us to understand.

To speak of eschatology is to raise the question of the biblical view of time itself as it relates to the fulfillment of the purposes of God. Prophetic eschatology and apocalyptic eschatology are radically different ways of understanding time in relation to salvation history.

The classical prophets of the OT understood time as linear, as a history of revelation and redemption. For them time had a beginning and an ending predetermined by the counsels of God alone. It is this concept of linear time that makes biblical eschatology possible. The prophetic understanding of time as linear is in marked contrast to the pagan nature cults whose view of time was cyclical, the expression of the annual agricultural cycle. In a cyclical conception of time there can be no eschatology. Pagan religions were consequently dedicated to maintaining, largely by mimetic magic, the unbroken rotation of the annual cycle. Any interruption of the agricultural cycle was viewed with the utmost alarm, for it signified famine and death. Because of its understanding of time as linear, the cultus of the OT sanctified time by celebrating God's redemptive acts in history. This understanding of time as linear is one of the truly momentous contributions of OT religion. Without it there would be no eschatology and no salvation history.

In the prophetic linear conception of history, time was regarded as the vehicle of God's saving purpose toward Israel, and the crucial events in the history of Israel mark a progression in time toward time's ultimate fulfillment, the ushering in of the kingdom of God. John the Baptist stood squarely in this prophetic linear view of eschatology. It is, therefore, within this time frame that his words and actions are to be interpreted.

In the later history of the Jewish people, from the Babylonian exile through the Roman domination of Judah, an increasing pessimism arose about the linear view of time and its ability to fulfill God's purposes. Devastating social and political convulsions, aggravated by foreign exploitation and oppression, led men to despair of time as a vehicle for the fulfillment of the theocratic hope. Rather than seeing history as working out the purposes of God, time and the course of human events were seen as thwarting the coming of the kingdom. Time itself must come, therefore, under divine judgment. In a final parousia, God would consequently terminate time. His cataclysmic invasion of time and space would usher in a new era of righteousness and justice, that is to say, the coming of the kingdom of heaven from heaven. It is this apocalyptic despair of time that distinguishes the eschatological discourses of Jesus during the Passion Week.

When, therefore, John's baptism in the Spirit and fire and the Pentecostal baptism in the Spirit for power-in-mission are juxtaposed, it is essential to distinguish the prophetic frame of reference appropriate to each. The application of this insight will play a significant role in the next chapter.

Notes

[1]James D. G. Dunn, *Baptism in the Holy Spirit* (1970; Rpt. Philadelphia: The Westminster Press, 1977), pp. 8–22.

[2]Ibid., pp. 21, 22.

[3]Ibid., pp. 13, 14.

[4]Unless noted otherwise, all biblical quotations are from the Revised Standard Version, abbr., RSV.

[5]*Commentary on the Book of the Acts* (Grand Rapids: Wm. B. Eerdmans Publishing Co., 1964), pp. 68, 69.

[6]Dunn, op. cit., pp. 21, 22.

Chapter 2

Jesus' Baptism in the Spirit

The next step in the development of the conversion-initiation paradigm is a discussion of the significance of Jesus' baptismal experience. Briefly stated, Dunn's premise is that Jesus' baptism in the Spirit at Jordan was primarily initiatory. This is clearly set forth in his own words:

Only with the descent of the Spirit does the new covenant and new epoch enter, and only thus does Jesus himself enter the new covenant and epoch. He enters as representative man—representing in himself Israel and even mankind. As such, this first baptism in the Spirit could well be taken as typical of all later Spirit-baptisms—the means by which God brings each to follow in Jesus' footsteps. Jesus as representative of the people (ὁ λαός— cf. Luke 2:10, 32; 3:21) is the first to enter the promise made to the people.[1]

The Pentecostal emphasis upon the baptism in the Spirit as primarily for power-in-mission is not denied. It is deftly relegated to a subordinate place. This too is clearly enunciated by the author.

At the same time, Pentecostals are right to recognize that Jesus'anointing with the Spirit was what equipped him for his messianic ministry of healing and teaching (Acts 10.38). This "empowering for service" should not however be taken as the primary purpose of the anointing—it is only a corollary to it. The baptism in the Spirit, in other words, is not primarily to equip the (already) Christian for service; rather its function is to initiate the individual into the new age and covenant, to "Christ" (= anoint) him, and in so doing to equip him for life and service in the new age and covenant. In this Jesus' entry into the new age and covenant is the type of every initiate's entry into the new age and covenant.[2]

In response to these allegations, it should be noted first of all that they are theological constructs. They are a logical extension of the basic assumptions of the conversion-initiation hypothesis. No hard exegetical evidence can be adduced to support them.

In the following analysis, it will be argued that: (1) The new covenant did not begin with the descent of the Spirit at Jordan. (2) Consequently, the anointing with the Spirit did not mark Jesus' entrance into the new covenant. (3) Jesus' baptism *is* typical of all subsequent Spirit-baptisms, not as initiatory, but for power-in-mission. (4) The only purpose for the baptism in the Spirit is empowerment for life and service.

Jesus' supernatural conception and subsequent baptism in the Holy Spirit at Jordan provide a theological paradigm for contemporary Pente-

5

costal experience and doctrine. The exegetical support for this paradigm will be explored in subsequent discussions.

As Jesus was supernaturally conceived by action of the Holy Spirit, so, too, Christians experience a supernatural rebirth through the same Holy Spirit. At the beginning of His public ministry, Jesus was anointed with the Holy Spirit, thus empowering Him for His ministry of preaching, teaching, and healing. Subsequently His disciples were baptized in the Holy Spirit at Pentecost for power in their lives and ministries. From the point of view of contemporary Pentecostal experience and exegesis, this establishes a pattern of spirituality operative today.

"The Experience of Jesus at Jordan"[3] is a vigorous rebuttal of the Pentecostal understanding of these events in the life of Jesus, according to Dunn. The reader is informed that "where the Pentecostalist thesis breaks down is in its failure to grasp the fact that we are dealing here with events whose significance, at least for those who record them, lies almost totally in the part they play in salvation-history."[4] The Pentecostal does not deny that the Jordan event occupies a significant place in salvation-history. What he does query is the gratuitous claim that it is the "pivot [on which] the whole of salvation-history swings round into a new course."[5]

Even more dubious is the supporting claim that "The experience of Jesus at Jordan is far more than something *merely* personal—it is a unique moment in history."[6] The qualifier "merely personal" has a pejorative ring to it. By innuendo the centrality of Jesus' personal experience is thereby denigrated without recourse to the context. In so doing, the clearly personal significance of the event for the experience of Jesus is deprecated, and with it, at least by implication, the emphasis placed upon it by the Pentecostal thesis as a paradigm for subsequent Christian experience.

In the context of the conversion-initiation hypothesis, the moment is unique in salvation-history because it marks the beginning of the new covenant and Jesus' entrance into the covenant. Its significance is, therefore, primarily initiatory. But such an allegation is gratuitous. A careful exegesis of the passage gives no hint that this is the intent of the Evangelist in recording the event. The events at Jordan marked the dénouement of the older covenant, not the beginning of the new. The new covenant could not begin until the old covenant had reached its finale.

Proleptically, the divine address from heaven reinforced Jesus' filial consciousness in view of His impending ordeal in the wilderness. The first temptation, "If you are the Son of God" (Luke 4:3, 9), challenged

Him at this very point. If, therefore, Jesus' filial consciousness is not central to the narrative, the temptation is an anomaly.

Thus when the Jordan experience of Jesus is related to its context, the details converge on one center, the filial consciousness of Jesus. Salvation-history and the personal experience of Jesus are indivisible. The uniqueness of Jesus' baptism in the Spirit resides in the fact that it establishes a precedent, not that it is unrepeatable. He was anointed with the Spirit for power for life and ministry. He who was thus baptized in the Spirit, baptized, in turn, His disciples on the day of Pentecost. Jesus' experience of Spirit-baptism does provide the paradigm that unites all subsequent experiences of Spirit-baptism with His in the history of salvation.

As the "pivot" of history, the Jordan event is further described as "the beginning of a new epoch in salvation-history—the beginning, albeit in a restricted sense, of the End-time, the messianic age, the new covenant"[7] One obvious objection to this statement is that it ignores Luke's identification of Joel's "last days" (Acts 2:17) with Pentecost, not with Jordan. In the preliminary remarks about prophetic eschatology and apocalyptic eschatology, these two stakes were driven in from which the eschatological landscape is to be surveyed. Before continuing this survey of the eschatological terrain, a methodological problem dictates a response.

On occasion categorical assertations in defense of the conversion-initiation thesis are hedged by such phrases as "albeit in a restricted sense." The qualification here tempers the dogmatic statements about the significance of the Jordan event with an aura of scholarly restraint. One is led thereby to anticipate an evenhanded treatment of all aspects of the subject. However, the ensuing discussion repeats these statements without benefit of qualifiers. In point of fact, this very paragraph ends with doctrinaire affirmations based upon these initial generalizations. It is asserted, for instance, that "It is in fact *the event* [apparently no longer 'in a restricted sense'] which begins the new covenant for Jesus—it initiates the messianic age and initiates Jesus into the messianic age."[8] As a result, such disclaimers are regarded as stylistic rather than substantive.

The ground has now been cleared for a critical evaluation of the claim that Jesus' reception of the Holy Spirit at Jordan is "the beginning . . . of the End-time, the messianic age, the new covenant." These are fundamental presuppositions upon which the theology of conversion-initiation rests.

In the Gospel of Mark, Jesus opened His public ministry by announcing that "The time (ὁ καιρός) is fulfilled, and the kingdom of God is at hand" (1:15). How then is ὁ καιρός to be understood? True, it is "one of the chief eschatological terms,"[9] but in what sense is eschatological time fulfilled? The answer given above is correct as far it goes. "The time of the End expected by the prophets has come in some sense at least,"[10] but failure to distinguish between the prophetic end-of-time and the apocalyptic time-of-the-end leads to the wrong conclusion.

"The time is fulfilled, and the kingdom of God is at hand," but not yet. The kingdom is offered but refused. The kingdom realized as the fulfillment of prophetic eschatology would not constitute "a decisive 'shift in the aeons.' "[11] It would be the logical outcome of the prophetic understanding of salvation-history as linear, and Jordan belongs to that former aeon, an aeon that did not run its course until the rejection and crucifixion of Jesus drastically altered the *eschaton*.

The context of the Jordan event belongs to prophetic rather than to apocalyptic eschatology. It is the conception of history as linear that predominates here. The Exodus, the Davidic dynasty, the fall of Jerusalem, the exile and restoration of Judah, the birth of Messiah, the Jordan event—all are bench marks in linear prophetic time pointing to the fulfillment of time and the kingdom at hand. And it is this view of eschatology that dominates the Gospels until Passion Week, and the apocalyptic discourses of Jesus drastically altered eschatological expectations.

Amidst the crises precipitated by the events of Passion Week, Jesus' End-time pronouncements no longer reflect the classical prophetic view of eschatology. His discourses in Matt. 24:1ff., Mark 13:1ff., and Luke 21:5ff. are marked by an apocalyptic pessimism. Rather than ushering in the kingdom, the times will become worse and worse. False christs, apostasy, false prophets, and lawlessness will mark the course of this age, but the end is not yet. Rather, the kingdom at hand in Mark 1:15 becomes the kingdom indefinitely postponed. Instead of ushering in the kingdom, time itself will be ended abruptly by a cosmic invasion of God and the advent of the Kingdom of Heaven from heaven.

However, before this apocalyptic finale, Jesus declared that "this gospel of the kingdom shall be preached in the whole world for a witness to all the nations, and then the end shall come" (Matt. 24:14, NASB).[12] The witness motif recurs in Acts 1:8, "you shall receive power when the Holy Spirit has come upon you; and you shall be My witnesses . . . to the end of the earth." That the witness embraced the gospel of the kingdom is clear from Paul's preaching, who, though a prisoner at Rome, "welcomed all who came to him, preaching the kingdom of God and teaching about the Lord Jesus Christ" (Acts 28:30, 31).

The common denominator between Matt. 24:14 and Acts 1:8 is Pentecost, not the coming of the Spirit upon Jesus at Jordan. The time frame is apocalyptic rather than prophetic eschatology. The *eschaton* is identified by the Evangelist with the Pentecostal effusion of the Spirit upon the disciples, not with Jesus' Spirit-baptism at Jordan.

Faced with the proclamation of Jesus that prophetic time was fulfilled, that the kingdom of God was imminent, His contemporaries had two options. First, to accept Him as the promised Messiah and, thus, realize the fulfillment of the kingdom. Second, to reject Him and in so doing to alter time itself as the vehicle of the coming of the kingdom. The categorical nature of His announcement left no other alternative.

With His rejection and crucifixion prophetic time was foreclosed. Henceforth, the redeemed wait for the King himself to descend from heaven "with a shout, with the voice of *the* archangel, and with the trumpet of God" (I Thess. 4:16, NASB).

The evidence adduced thus far is sufficiently weighty to reject the claim that the experience of Jesus at Jordan is "the beginning [even in a restricted sense] of the End-time." The Jordan experience of Jesus belongs to the fulfillment of prophetic time. Pentecost ushered in the apocalyptic End-time.

What now of the claim that the Jordan event as the "pivot" of history is the beginning of "the messianic age, the new covenant?" The nativity stories mark the Incarnation as the beginning of the messianic age. The witness of the nativity narratives cannot be rendered innocuous by a nuanced concession, "There is a sense in which Jesus is Messiah and Son of God from his birth ([Luke] 1:35, 43, 76; 2:11, 26, 49)."[13] It is the only sense in which He is the Messiah and Son of God, "for to you is born this day in the city of David a Saviour, who is Christ [= Messiah] the Lord" (Luke 2:11). Subsequent references in the Gospels to His messianic identity (Matt. 16:16; John 11:27) are more naturally and consistently related to the nativity account than to the Jordan episode.

What is explicitly affirmed in the context of the Jordan account is the connection between Jesus' Spirit-baptism and His empowerment for ministry. This is acknowledged in a passing remark, "We certainly cannot deny that it was this anointing with the Spirit which equipped Jesus with power and authority for his mission to follow (Acts

10:38).''[14] This acknowledgement translates further on into a concession that ''Pentecostals are right to recognize that Jesus' anointing with the Spirit was what equipped him for his messianic ministry of healing and teaching.'' The concession is hedged immediately, however, with a disclaimer, ''This 'empowering for service' should not however be taken as a primary purpose of the anointing—it is only a corollary to it.''[15] But this assertion is in obvious contradiction to the textual evidence. The only purpose attributed by the Evangelist to the anointing with the Spirit is empowerment for service (cf. Acts 1:8).

The exegetical and theological inadequacies of the conversion-initiation hypothesis become evident at this point. Textual evidence for the initiatory significance of the baptism in the Spirit is conspicuously absent.[16] Hard evidence that the baptism in the Spirit is for power-in-mission is clearly attested.

After His baptism in the Spirit, ''Jesus, full of the Holy Spirit'' (Luke 4:1), faced the tempter in the wilderness. Jesus returned victorious ''in the power of the Spirit into Galilee'' (Luke 4:14). Entering the synagogue at Nazareth, He selected for His text Isaiah 61:1f. ''The Spirit of the Lord is upon me, because he has anointed me to preach . . . '' (Luke 4:18). The corollary with Acts 10:38 is obvious. In Capernaum the authority of His words, and His power to exorcise demons was greeted with amazement by the congregation in the synagogue (Luke 4:36). On another occasion, as He taught in the presence of the Pharisees and teachers of the law, ''the power of the Lord was with him to heal'' (Luke 5:17). On yet another occasion, as the crowd pressed upon Him to touch Him, ''power came forth from him and healed them all'' (Luke 6:19).

It requires some theological ingenuity to identify the baptism in the Spirit with conversion-initiation, but were the theme of power in service removed from Luke/Acts, its message would be largely unintelligible.

Given the explicit correlation between Jesus' baptism in the Spirit and power-in-mission, the assertion that ''the Baptism in the Spirit, as always, is primarily initiatory and only secondarily an empowering,''[17] must be rejected as lacking hard exegetical evidence to support it. The Evangelist himself does not leave the reader to grope for the meaning of the events that occurred at the Jordan. The free quotation of the Septuagint version of Isaiah 61:1–2 by Jesus is the interpretation:

The Spirit of the Lord is upon me, because he has anointed me to preach good news to the poor. He has sent me to proclaim release to the captives and recovering of sight to the blind, to set at liberty those who are oppressed, to proclaim the acceptable year of the Lord (Luke 4:18, 19).

The original intention of the prophet could not have been lost upon Luke, nor upon Jesus who appropriated the passage to interpret His Jordan experience in the light of the prophet's words, "Today this scripture has been fulfilled in your hearing" (Luke 4:21). Jordan was Jesus' consecration to prophetic ministry.

The coming of the Spirit "upon" the OT prophet signified His consecration and empowerment to fulfill the prophetic office to which He had been called. It was the Spirit's presence and power that enabled the prophet to proclaim the oracles of Yahweh. Jesus, in appropriating the words of the OT prophet for himself, identified His baptism in the Spirit as empowerment for a prophetic ministry.

Excursus on Jesus, Son and Messiah

The identification of the Jordan event with "the beginning . . . of the messianic age,"[18] raises "the vexed question of the messiahship of Jesus and the bearing of this event on it."[19] The question is a christological question of the first magnitude, and according to the author of the above, is "often posed thus: Was the descent of the Spirit the moment of Jesus' adoption as Son of God and appointment as Messiah, or merely the climax and confirmation of a growing conviction that he was Son and Messiah?"[20]

If, as the author says, the question is a vexed one, then it is further complicated by combining indiscriminately an ontological category, *sonship,* and a functional category, *messiahship.* The anointing with the Spirit at Jordan for *messianic ministry* is not adoptionist in the strict sense of the word. However, to ask if the descent of the Spirit was "the moment of Jesus' adoption as Son of God," is baldly adoptionist. The alternate suggestion that it was a growing conviction of His sonship and messiahship may be referred to the prior discussion of Jesus' filial and messianic self-consciousness.

Any adoptionist claims for Luke's use of Psalm 2:7 in the context of the Jordan baptismal narrative faces a serious challenge from the text itself. The first such difficulty is the omission of the second stich of the verse, "this day have I begotten you," from all three of the synoptic accounts.[21] This must represent a formidable obstacle to an adoptionist Christology.

Another difficulty is the use of the full text of Psalm 2:7 in Acts 13:33 in the context of the resurrection. By the resurrection, Jesus in Romans 1:4 "has been declared [τοῦ ὁρισθέντος] to be the powerful Son of God."[22] The mystery of the divine Sonship is openly revealed for all to see and understand by the resurrection. He did not become the Son by resurrection. The resurrection is the incontrovertible proof of His Sonship. Orthodox Christianity did not, and does not, interpret the resurrection as adoption to Sonship in any sense. Adoption is a category predicated of Christians, but never of Jesus Christ. He is Son of God by nature; we become sons of God by grace.

The conclusion is self-evident. To invoke an adoptionist Christology to explain the experience of Jesus at Jordan is to leave the conversion-initiation hypothesis stranded on the shoals of heterodoxy.

A third obstacle to an adoptionist Christology here is the explicit contradiction of the Lukan nativity narrative that it produces. Dunn is alert to the potential contradiction and tries to resolve it by recourse to "the movement of salvation-history."[23] This argument must, therefore, be analyzed in some detail.

The crux of the argument from salvation-history is the following assertion:

> There is also a sense in which Jesus is Messiah and Son of God from his birth (1.35, 43, 76; 2.11, 26, 49); but there is also a sense in which he only becomes Messiah and Son at Jordan [shades of Certhinian Gnosticism], since he does not in fact become the Anointed One (Messiah) till then (Isa. 61. 1–2; Luke 4.18; Acts 10.38), and only then does the heavenly voice hail him as Son; just as there is a sense in which he does not become Messiah and Son till his resurrection and ascension (Acts 2.36; 13.33).[24]

With few exceptions, Pentecostals would affirm the orthodox view of the Incarnation. Jesus is the Son of God by nature. He never was, is not, and never will be other than the Son of God. For this very reason, the statement that "there is a sense in which Jesus is Messiah and Son of God from his birth" cannot be accepted without qualification. This is the *only sense* in which He is the Son of God. There is *no sense* in which Jesus "only becomes" Messiah and *Son* at Jordan. This is a category mistake. The same predicates cannot be ascribed univocally to the ontological category, *sonship*, and the functional category, *messiahship*. Jesus is Son of God by nature. He is Messiah by vocation.

Given the author's interpretation of salvation-history and allowing, for the sake of argument, the word play anoint = Christ (Χριστός), it may be permissible to say that Jesus becomes the Messiah through His anointing with the Spirit at Jordan. The predicate is then purely functional. But, the functional predicate, Messiah, cannot be attributed univocally to the category of Son. Sonship, in the context of the Lukan nativity narratives, can be interpreted only ontologically. There is, therefore, no sense in which Jesus "only becomes" at Jordan what He already is at Bethlehem. The predicate *being* may be attributed to His sonship which is by nature. The predicate *becoming* may be ascribed to His messiahship which is by vocation. They cannot be reversed, nor can they be conflated.

The appeal to salvation-history is, therefore, an attempt to shift the focus of the argument wholly to the functional level. This is tacitly admitted by a subsequent affirmation, "At each new phase of salvation-history Jesus enters upon a new and fuller phase of this messiahship and sonship."[25] But, this simply compounds the category mistake, leaving the entire argument vulnerable to the charge of adoptionism, and thereby prejudices the very foundations of the conversion-initiation paradigm.

Finally, as the "pivot" of history, can the Jordan event be described as the beginning of "the new covenant?" Negatively, it may be pointed out that nothing in the baptismal motif at Jordan even remotely suggests the new covenant. As a matter of fact, the only direct reference to covenant in the context is found, not in the Jordan event, but in the prophecy of Zacharias in the context of the nativity narrative, and there it refers to the old covenant.

As shown in the discussion of prophetic eschatology, what is in view in the Jordan account is the imminent dénouement of salvation-history as envisioned by the classical prophets of the OT. It is not yet the beginning of a new age but, the time of fulfillment of the old epoch, "the kingdom is at hand," but not yet.

In fact, the new covenant is not mentioned by any of the Evangelists until the close of Jesus' ministry. With His rejection and crucifixion, the prospect of the immediate emergence of the kingdom upon the world scene is foreclosed. It is in this context that the words of institution at the Last Supper signal the beginning of a new epoch, the new covenant. These same words of institution present a formidable obstacle to the claim that Jordan marked the beginning of the new covenant. The expression, "the new covenant in my blood," (ἡ καινὴ διαθήκη ἐν τῷ αἵματί μου, Luke 22:20) provides a chronological datum that an anti-sacramental bias seems to have obscured in the discussion.

There is no covenant without the shedding of the blood of the sacrificial victim. Thus the old covenant, sealed with sacrificial blood, was in effect until the death of Jesus. He in turn is the sacrificial lamb of the new covenant. It was in sign that Jesus, as our high priest, offered himself at the last Passover in the words of institution. The new covenant could be initiated only by action of Jesus in His role as high priest, who "through his own blood, He entered the holy place once and for all, having obtained eternal redemption" (Heb. 9:12). Jordan is not an altar; the cross is, and it is at the altar that the new covenant is initiated.

Notes

[1]Dunn, op. cit., 32.
[2]Ibid.
[3]Ibid., pp. 23-37.
[4]Ibid., p. 24.
[5]Ibid.
[6]Ibid., italics added.
[7]Ibid.
[8]Ibid., p. 25, italics added.
[9]Walter Bauer, William F. Arndt, and F. Wilbur Gingrich, *Greek-English Lexicon of the New Testament* (Chicago: The University of Chicago Press, 1957).
[10]Dunn, op. cit., p. 26.
[11]Ibid.
[12]New American Standard Bible, abbr. NASB.
[13]Dunn, op. cit., p. 28.
[14]Ibid., p. 24.
[15]Ibid., p. 32.
[16]The one apparent exception, I Cor. 12:13, will be addressed later.
[17]Dunn, op. cit., p. 54.
[18]Ibid., p. 24.
[19]Ibid., pp. 27, 28.
[20]Ibid.
[21]Textual support for the second stich, ἐγὼ σήμερον γεγέννηκά σε, is found only in Luke 3:22 D, it, Ju, (Cl), Or. *Novum Testamentum Graece*, eds. Erwin Nestle et Kurt Aland 25th ed., (Stuttgart: Würtembergische Bibelanstalt, 1963).
[22]Bauer, Arndt, Gingrich.
[23]Dunn, op. cit., pp. 28, 29.
[24]Ibid.
[25]Ibid.

Chapter 3

Pentecost

What Jordan was to Jesus, Pentecost was to the disciples. As Jesus entered the new age and covenant by being baptized in the Spirit at Jordan, so the disciples followed him in like manner at Pentecost.[1]

This constitutes the thesis of "The Miracle of Pentecost."[2]

In rebuttal, it will be urged that: (1) The identification of Pentecost with the beginning of the new age and covenant violates the covenantal presuppositions of both testaments. (2) The absence of water baptism in the Pentecost context argues against the conversion-initiation paradigm. (3) If, in the logic of the conversion-initiation hypothesis, Pentecost was to the disciples what Jordan was to Jesus, then Pentecost cannot be construed as their new birth.

Once again the discussion is introduced with a strongly worded anti-Pentecostal and anti-Catholic bias. "When we look at Pentecost in the context of Luke/Acts it becomes evident that Pentecostal and Catholic alike have again missed the principal significance of the story."[3]

What then is "the principal significance of the story?" The fundamental thesis of the chapter is repeated over and over again. For instance, "the new age and covenant does not begin for the disciples until Pentecost."[4] It is affirmed again that "For Luke Pentecost is also the beginning of the new covenant for the disciples."[5] With a slight variation on the theme, "Pentecost inaugurates the age of the Church . . . and is 'the beginning of the period of the Church.'"[6] The latter statement is reinforced with the dogmatic assertion that "the Church properly conceived did not come into existence until Pentecost; . . . there were no Christians (properly speaking) prior to Pentecost."[7]

We do not belabor the point, but simply point out that, if this thesis can be shown to be wrong in one context, multiple repetitions do not make it right.

The qualifications "properly conceived" and "(properly speaking)" have the ring of special pleading. Apparently the Church can be "properly conceived" only within the conversion-initiation paradigm.

The comment that "there were no Christians (properly speaking) prior to Pentecost" prompts a digression. In the strictest sense of the word, Christians are not characterized as such until the apostolic witness reached Antioch, where "the disciples were for the first time called Christians" (Acts 11:26). Initially, the disciples of Jesus were regarded as Jews, hardly distinguishable from a number of other sects in Judaism. With the opening of the fellowship to Gentiles at Antioch, they were identified as a messianic sect of dubious orthodoxy. They were apparently still regarded as a Jewish sect, however, within the broad spectrum of Diaspora Judaism, but with a taint of heterodoxy associated with the circumcision controversy.

Addressing now the thesis of "The Miracle of Pentecost," three observations may be made in response to its basic assumption.

1. The assertion that "the new age and covenant does not begin for the disciples until Pentecost" creates an insuperable theological problem. The efficacy of the Mosaic covenant ceased with the death of Jesus. Jesus announced the beginning of the new covenant in the words of institution at the Last Supper, i.e., "the new covenant in my blood" (Matt. 26:28; Mark 14:24; Luke 22;20; I Cor. 11:25). If one is looking for "watersheds" in salvation-history, it is strange that this one is overlooked.

It is a basic presupposition of both testaments that a covenant is indispensable for the relationship of God with His covenant people. Until the death of Jesus His disciples had their relationship with, and access to, God under the terms of the old covenant. If, therefore, the new covenant did not begin for the disciples until Pentecost, and the old covenant was terminated fifty days earlier at Passover, then the disciples were without covenant relationship with God from Passover to Pentecost. Such a conclusion would violate the basic covenantal presuppositions of both the OT and the NT. It is a contradiction that defies satisfactory resolution, unless one is prepared to accept the Paschal impartation of the Holy Spirit to Jesus' disciples on the evening of the resurrection day (John 20:22) as their "new birth," and entry into the new covenant.

2. The claim that "there were no Christians (properly speaking) prior to Pentecost" makes Pentecost a conversion-initiation experience for Jesus' disciples. This is clearly enunciated in the statement that it is "only when Jesus has been exalted that they are initiated into the new covenant by receiving the Spirit."[8] It is articulated again in a concluding remark, "The Baptism in the Spirit, as always, is primarily initiatory."[9]

This conclusion is flawed, however, by the fact that whenever the baptism in /filling with/ the gift of the Holy Spirit is recorded in Acts in context with a conversion experience, water baptism is an indispensable part of conversion and initiation, with one exception, viz., Pentecost.

It may be argued, therefore, that the absence of water baptism in the Pentecost narrative is inductive evidence that the Pentecostal baptism in the Spirit was not a conversion-initiation experience for the disciples. This does not argue, however, that the 120 disciples present at Pentecost had not been baptized previously. On the contrary, there are hints in the Gospels that point toward an earlier initiation into discipleship. Some of Jesus' disciples had experienced the baptism of John before transferring their allegiance to Jesus. For John, and for Jesus, discipleship and baptism were practically synonymous. Jesus himself baptized (John 3:22–26), though not personally (John 4:1, 2), and taught His disciples to baptize (Matt. 28:19; Mark 16:16).

Furthermore, since Jesus called upon converts to "repent, and believe in the gospel" of the kingdom (Mark 1:14, 15), it is not unreasonable to deduce that these were preconditions to their baptism. On these terms, it can be argued that their conversion and initiation into discipleship preceded, and was a precondition of, the Paschal insufflation of the Holy Spirit and could thereby explain why baptism is noticeable by its absence from the context.

3. If, furthermore, "there were no Christians (properly speaking) prior to Pentecost,"[10] then the reception of the Holy Spirit at Pentecost is tantamount to their "new birth from above" (John 3:3). Although not spelled out this precisely, it is nonetheless implied in the statement, "Where up till then only Jesus had experienced life in the new age, now they too can experience that life—for they share in his life."[11] The statement is ambiguous, and in the light of the discussion of "The Experience of Jesus at Jordan," the ambiguity raises justifiable misgivings. Does this imply that Jesus' experience of "life in the new age" corresponded to their "new birth from above?" Put another way, was Jordan a "new birth" experience for Jesus? If not, wherein is the correspondence? If so, does it not raise again the specter of adoptionism, for it was categorically stated that there is "a sense in which he only becomes . . . Son at Jordan."[12]

Be that as it may, the onus rests upon the conversion-initiation thesis to demonstrate that Pentecost resulted in the new birth for the disciples. Only thus could it be said that the Church came into existence at Pentecost. In the context of the Acts, the only predicate attributed to the baptism in the Spirit is that "you shall receive power" (Acts 1:8). The categorical pronouncement that "the phrase 'baptism in Spirit' is never directly associated with the promise of power, but is always associated with entry into the messianic age or the Body of Christ"[13] is a surprising error of fact. The factual error in this assertion is sufficient in and of itself to discredit the entire conversion-initiation hypothesis.

The fundamental thesis of "The Miracle of Pentecost" is defended by a "threefold scheme of salvation-history."[14] In the total scheme of Luke/Acts, Luke is said to interpret history in three phases, viz., "the period of Israel, the period of Jesus, and the period between the coming of Jesus and his parousia."[15] In the development of this scheme of salvation-history, each phase is inaugurated by Jesus' entrance into a new relationship with the Spirit: (1) at His incarnation, (2) at His anointing with the Spirit at Jordan, and (3) finally having received the promise of the Spirit after His ascension, He poured out the Spirit upon his disciples. His submission to John's baptism "triggered off" the transition from the first to the second; His submission to the baptism of the cross effected the transition from the second to the third.[16]

The paradigm has an almost homiletical symmetry, but like all too many sermons, it subordinates substance to rhetorical form. From the eschatological perspective "the period of Israel" and "the period of Jesus" are one and the same. Jesus interpreted His own ministry as a continuation and fulfillment of the prophetic ministry of Isaiah (Luke 4:21). From the covenantal perspective also, "the period of Israel" and "the period of Jesus" are one, for the old covenant did not end until the rejection and crucifixion of Jesus. If one were to categorize it more precisely, it can be said that "the period of Israel" ended during the Passion Week with Jesus' pronouncement of judgment upon Israel, "Therefore I tell you, the kingdom of God will be taken away from you and given to a nation producing the fruits of it" (Matt. 21:43).

The failure of John's expectation of the imminent end of the age in a messianic baptism of Spirit and fire is explained by recourse to "Luke's twofold understanding of the events of Jordan."[17]

The first of these is "Jesus *own* entry into the new age and covenant" through the descent of the Spirit at Jordan.[18] The rebuttal is, or ought to be, obvious. The context does not interpret the coming of the Spirit upon Jesus as His entry into the new age and covenant. In Jesus' own understanding it was ordination to prophetic ministry (Luke 4:18f.). Thereby He identified His mission with that of Isaiah, the representative man of the Spirit of the old covenant. At Jordan OT messianic prophecy and promise reached its culmination in Jesus. There is no sense in which the context indicates entry into the new covenant at Jordan. Its ambience is that of Israel and the old covenant. The new covenant did not begin even proleptically for Him, or for anyone else, before His announcement of it at the Last Supper.

"The second aspect of Jesus' experience at Jordan," so it is claimed, ". . . was also his anointing with the Spirit as Messiah and Servant."[19] He became thereby both Servant and Representative for His people. Consequently, for Luke the culmination of Jesus' work as Messiah and Servant and Representative was the cross "where Jesus accepted and endured the messianic baptism in Spirit-and-fire on behalf of his people."[20] Luke 12:49f. is identified as the key passage since both concepts of "fire" and "baptism" occur in it.

I came to cast fire on the earth; and would that
  it were already kindled!
I have a baptism to be baptized with; and how I
  am constrained until it is accomplished!

The force of the argument here rests upon the assertion that "These two verses are undoubtedly to be taken as parallel members of the one idea."[21]

Two assumptions are made here that are open to dispute. (1) The "fire" of John's eschatological baptism equals the fire that Jesus came to cast upon the earth. (2) The assumed parallelism between "fire" and "baptism" in Luke 12:49f. supports the first assumption.

In light of the context, these assumptions are simply category mistakes. The "fire" of v. 49 is not equated contextually with John's eschatological baptism in fire. It is not the "unquenchable fire" that burns up the chaff (Luke 3:17). It is a "fire" that brings sharp divisions even within families for the sake of Christ. In a parallel saying, it is persecution endured for the sake of Jesus and His gospel (Matt. 10:34–36). The ideas of "fire" and "baptism" in the Lukan context are not parallel; they reflect instead a causal connection. The "fire" of division and persecution is the consequence of His "baptism" at the cross.

The cross was not "the messianic baptism in Spirit-and-fire." Jordan was Jesus' baptism in the Spirit. The cross was His baptism of redemptive fire. The two cannot be conflated.

Excursus on ἡ ἐπαγγελία: Luke 24:49; Acts 1:4; 2:33, 38–39

A final word is in order in response to the contention that "For Luke Pentecost is also the beginning of the new covenant for the disciples."[22] In support of this claim, it is noted that the Spirit which is given to them is referred to four times as ἡ ἐπαγγελία, (*the promise*, Luke 24:49; Acts 1:4; 2:33, 38f.), "a word often used by both Paul and Luke to characterize the covenant promise of God to his people"[23] However, no effort is made to demonstrate that it is used in this sense in the four Lukan passages cited. The fundamental error in the argument here rests with the assumption that Luke and Paul use the word univocally, that is, in one sense only, rather than equivocally, that is in more than one sense as dictated by the context.

Upon closer examination neither the texts nor the contexts identify ἡ ἐπαγγελία in the broad sense of "the covenant promise of God to his people." The focus of the context is quite specific. In Luke 24:49 "the promise of my Father" is expressly defined as "clothed with power from on high." The same correlation is made between "the promise of the Father" and the baptism in the Holy Spirit for power-in-mission (Acts 1:4, 5, 8). In the context of the Pentecost narrative there is no evidence that would suggest any other meaning in Acts 2:33, 38. Contextually, "the promise of the Holy Spirit" received from the Father and poured out "in this which you see and hear" (2:33) is the coming of the Spirit in His charisms of power-in-mission.

A cursory survey of the Greek concordance[24] makes it obvious that both Luke and Paul use the expression in more than one sense. For this reason, the citation of texts cannot be lumped together indiscriminately. The meaning must first be determined from each context.

A case in point is the citation of Gal. 3:14 in support of the assertion that ἡ ἐπαγγελία is "a word often used by Paul and by Luke to characterize the covenant promise of God to his people."[25] But, is this what the word means in the context of Gal. 3:14? The text reads, "that in Christ Jesus the blessing of Abraham might come upon the Gentiles, that we might receive the promise (τήν ἐπαγγελίαν) of the Spirit through faith."

Verse 14 is the answer to Paul's rhetorical question in v. 2, "Did you receive the Spirit by the works of the law, or by the hearing with faith (ἢ ἐξ ἀκοῆς πίστεως)?" Πίστεως is here a subjective genitive, the hearing "which comes of faith."[26] "Faith," in the context, is a precondition for "hearing." "Hearing" precedes the reception of the Spirit.

The sense in which "the promise of the Spirit" (v. 14) is intended here is made clear from v. 5, "Does he who supplies (ἐπιχορηγῶν, present participle) the Spirit to you and works (ἐνεργῶν, present participle) miracles among you do so by the works of the law, or by the hearing of faith (ἢ ἐξ ἀκοῆς)?" The two present participles indicate the continuous manifestation of the Spirit's charisms in their midst. A paraphrase of v. 2 sharpens the sense of it, "Did you receive the gifts of faith?"

The blessing of Abraham (3:14) is the faith of Abraham that "was reckoned to him as righteousness" (3:16). It is in turn "men of faith who are the sons of Abraham" (3:7). In Christ, therefore, the Gentiles receive the blessing of Abraham through faith "that we might receive (ἵνα λάβωμεν, final purpose clause) the promise of the Spirit through faith" (3:14). In other words, "that we might receive the promised gifts of the Spirit through faith."

We do not receive the promise of the Spirit in order to receive the blessing of Abraham (the conversion-initiation thesis), but we receive the blessing of Abraham in order (ἵνα with the subjunctive λάβωμεν) to receive the promised Holy Spirit (the Pentecostal view). As in the texts already cited, Luke 24:49; Acts 1:4; 2:33, 38f., the promise of the Spirit in Gal. 3:14 is power-in-mission, not entrance into the new covenant. Thus, Gal. 3:14 may be claimed to support the Pentecostal point of view.

This leads to the conclusion that the use of ἡ ἐπαγγελία by Luke in the Pentecost narrative does not support the contention that "For Luke Pentecost is also the beginning of the new covenant for the disciples."[27]

Excursus on Acts 2:38

For the conversion-initiation hypothesis, Acts 2:38 is pivotal, "And Peter said to them, 'Repent, and be baptized everyone of you in the name of Jesus Christ for the forgiveness of your sins; and you shall receive the gift of the Holy Spirit.'"

The following remark reflects clearly the importance of this text for this hypothesis, "Luke probably intends Acts 2:38 to establish the pattern and norm for Christian conversion-initiation in his presentation of Christianity's beginnings."[28]

One may indeed speculate whether or not there could have been a conversion-initiation hypothesis without it. Be that as it may, it is accorded primacy of place in the advocacy of this thesis. This much is acknowledged in the affirmation that

Furthermore, it is the only verse in Acts which directly relates to one another the three most important elements in conversion-initiation: repentance, water-baptism, and the gift of the Spirit—repentance and faith being the opposite sides of the same coin.[29]

In other words, one is not a Christian until he has experienced all the elements of the conversion-initiation paradigm "whose unity cannot be broken."[30]

Wherein then does the Pentecostal view differ from this synthesis? In the Pentecostal understanding repentance/faith and water baptism constitute conversion and initiation. The Spirit is active in repentance and faith, and this activity is coterminous with regeneration. As a matter of fact, there can be neither faith nor repentance without the direct agency of the Holy Spirit. The baptism in /filling with/ gift of the Holy Spirit is, therefore, subsequent to conversion and initiation. As for the role of water baptism in conversion and initiation, many Pentecostals, although by no means all of them, would agree with the added dictum of the conversion-initiation thesis, water baptism is symbolic.

In the conversion-initiation thesis, the baptism in /filling with/ gift of the Holy Spirit is conflated with the Spirit's regenerative action (John 3:3, 5; I Peter 1:23; et al.). In a Pentecostal understanding of spiritual rebirth, it is, by its very nature, observable only in and through a changed life. It is characterized by the fruit(s) of the Spirit (Gal. 5:22). On the other hand, in Acts the gift of the Spirit is manifested in the Spirit's charisms; for example, tongues, prophecy, healings, et al. The distinction is a substantive one, and the failure of the conversion-initiation hypothesis to address it convincingly is a serious weakness.

An obvious question confronts the reader in the claim that Acts 2:38 establishes "the pattern and norm for Christian conversion-initiation." Does the context bear out this assumption? Verse 41 records in part the response to Peter's admonition, "So those who received his word (ἀποδεξάμενοι) were baptized (ἐβαπτίσθησαν), and there were added (προσετέθηοαν [i.e., to the Church]) that day about three thousand souls," They received the word, were baptized, and were added to the Church—with no mention of the gift of the Spirit! In fact, the next reference to the filling with /the gift of the Spirit does not occur until Acts 4:8, 31, and that in a context that is *not* a conversion-initiation context. This must represent an anomaly for the conversion-initiation theory, to say the least.

Of course, it may be argued that the gift of the Spirit is implied in 2:41f., but this is an appeal to propositional logic rather than to a clearly demonstrable exegetical datum. It is simply an acknowledgement that the conversion-initiation schema is not clearly articulated in Luke/Acts. It is a logical construct. This fact is at times lost sight of in the rhetoric with which it is advocated. But is not the Pentecostal position vulnerable to the same charge? Certainly, the Pentecostal thesis is not devoid of its own appeal to logic. It is not the emotional, irrational phenomenon some of its more radical critics have perceived it to be.

The real question at issue here is a methodological one. Both the conversion-initiation and the Pentecostal advocates appeal to Scripture and to logic. Both make certain hermeneutical assumptions and employ theological and exegetical criteria within the context of those assumptions. A fundamental difference, however, is the added appeal of the Pentecostal witness to a personal experience with the charisms of the Spirit subsequent to conversion. This appeal to a "Pentecostal" experience does not preempt the first two criteria but is understood as a corroborative witness to the biblical integrity of the Pentecostal thesis.

Notes

[1]Dunn, op. cit., p. 40.
[2]Ibid., pp. 38–54.
[3]Ibid., p. 40.
[4]Ibid., p. 43.
[5]Ibid., p. 47.
[6]Ibid., p. 49.
[7]Ibid., p. 51.
[8]Ibid., p. 43.
[9]Ibid., p. 54.
[10]Ibid., p. 51.
[11]Ibid., p. 43.
[12]Ibid., p. 28.
[13]Ibid., p. 54.
[14]Ibid., p. 41.
[15]Ibid., p. 40.
[16]Ibid., pp. 40–41.
[17]Ibid., p. 41.
[18]Ibid.
[19]Ibid., pp. 41, 42.
[20]Ibid., p. 42.
[21]Ibid., p. 42.
[22]Ibid., p. 47.
[23]Ibid.
[24]W. F. Moulton and A. S. Geden, *A Concordance to the Greek Testament* (1897; rpt. Edinburgh: T. & T. Clark, 1967).
[25]Dunn, op. cit., p. 47.
[26]J. B. Lightfoot, *Saint Paul's Epistle to the Galatians* (London: Macmillan and Co., 1896), p. 135.
[27]Dunn, op. cit., p. 47.
[28]Ibid., p. 90.
[29]Ibid., p. 91.
[30]Ibid., p. 221.

Chapter 4

Samaria, Riddle or Pattern of Pentecost?

According to the conversion-initiation hypothesis, even though the Samaritans had *believed* and been *baptized* (Acts 8:12), they were not Christians. They had not yet received the Holy Spirit (Acts 8:16f.) How then is their faith to be interpreted? The faith of the Samaritan converts is said to be defective, scarcely more than a superstitious credulity. The principal exegetical proof offered in support of these assumptions is a discussion of πιστεύειν ("to believe") with a dative object.

In rebuttal, it will be shown that this reconstruction of the data is special pleading, bolstered by a forced exegesis and unfounded speculation.

"The Riddle of Samaria"[1] is introduced by a reference to Acts 8 as "the chief stronghold of Pentecostal (baptism in the Spirit) and Catholic (Confirmation) alike."[2] The statement is something less than completely accurate. The Pentecostal position is not so vulnerable that a theological or linguistic tour de force at its "chief stronghold" could devastate its entire hermeneutic.[3]

The case for the conversion-initiation thesis may be summarized in the author's own words.

The problem of Acts 8 centres on two facts: the Samaritans believed and were baptized; they did not receive the Spirit until some time later. The problem is that in the context of the rest of the NT these facts appear to be mutually exclusive and wholly irreconcilable. If they believed and were baptized (v.12) in the name of the Lord Jesus (v. 16) they must be called Christians. But if they did not receive the Holy Spirit till later they cannot be called Christians until that time (most explicitly Rom. 8.9).[4]

The appeal to "the rest of the NT . . . (most explicitly Rom. 8.9)" entangles the argument in a methodological contradiction. In contrasting the methodology of the systematic theologian with the biblical theologian and exegete, the author himself stressed the following exegetical principle:

The method of the latter is to take each author and book separately and to (attempt to) outline his or its particular theological emphases; only when he has set a text in the context of its author's thought and intention (as expressed in his writing), only then can the biblical-theologian feel free to let that text interact with other texts from other books.[5]

Thus the indiscriminate appeal to "the rest of the NT . . . (most explicitly Rom. 8.9)," without first determining the meaning of specific texts "in the context of its author's thought," is a contradiction of the author's own hermeneutical principle. Furthermore, the identification of Rom. 8:9 as the Achilles' heel of the Pentecostal hermeneutic is a common device of anti-Pentecostal polemics. That is to say, "Anyone who does not have the Spirit of Christ does not belong to him." But the Pentecostal replies that the text has a context, and the context is not the Pentecostal baptism in the Holy Spirit.

In the context of Rom. 8, Paul draws a contrast between those "who are in the flesh" (v.8) which is *death*, with those who are "in the Spirit," that is to say, in whom "the Spirit of God dwells" (v. 9) which is spiritual *life* (v. 10, NASB).

What is assumed in the appeal to Rom. 8:9, but which is neither proved nor is it self-evident, is that this is identical with Luke's "you shall receive power when the Holy Spirit has come upon you; and you shall be my witnesses" (Acts 1:8). The burden of proof here rests with those who hold the view that "the Spirit of God dwell(ing) in you" = life (Paul) is identical with "the Spirit com(ing) upon you" = power-in-mission (Luke).

Clearly, there is a distinction in the Spirit's role, for *life* "through his Spirit which dwells in you" is ontological, while power-in-mission, "you shall be my witnesses," is phenomenological. The Pentecostal on both a contextual and an experiential basis would reject confusing the two. Life "in the Spirit" produces a change of identity—"he is a new creation" (II Cor. 5:17). Its only evidence scripturally and phenomenologically is the "fruit(s) of the Spirit" (Gal, 5:22), the attributes of the new (divine) nature in which the believer participates (II Peter 1:4).

On the other hand, the power manifested by the baptism in the Spirit is evidenced phenomenologically in tongues, prophecy, healings, etc.

Rom. 8:9 is concerned with the first experience of conversion and new birth by the Holy Spirit. It does not refer to the subsequent experience of the baptism in the Spirit for power-in-mission. Hence, Rom. 8:9 does not explain (or explain away) the laying on of hands by the apostles upon the Samaritans to receive the Holy Spirit. That this is so is borne out by the charismatic manifestations of the Spirit implied in v.

18. Thus, the conclusions of the conversion-initiation thesis do not proceed from an exegesis of the Samaritan experience in Acts 8 which are then shown to be compatible with Pauline theology, but Paul's theology, out of another context, preempts an exegesis of the phenomenology of Acts 8.

The Pentecostal hermeneutic, on the other hand, is consistent with the interpretative principle enunciated by Professor Dunn in the quotation above. Pentecostal exegesis begins with the phenomenology of Acts which the Pentecostal exegete sees as recapitulated in his own "Pentecostal" experience. This approach is consistent with the biblical pattern in which spiritual experience precedes reflection on the interpretation of the event. The point at issue here is whether the phenomenology of Spirit-baptism is to be interpreted by Pauline texts out of context, or whether Paul's theology is to be interpreted by the phenomenology of his own "Pentecostal" experience.

For the Pentecostal, whose Spirit-baptism-filling with the Spirit informs his application of critical, contextual exegesis, the fallacy of the anti-Pentecostal argument is that it interprets Paul's words propositionally, divorced from his experience. The theology of Spirit-baptism is thus reduced to the manipulation of conceptual constructs separated from the existential experience of those who lived the experience. In appealing legitimately to Rom. 8:9, one must first consider the phenomenology of Paul's experience in Acts 9:1–18; Rom. 15:19; and I Cor. 14:15–18.

The crucial text in the understanding of the experience of the Samaritans is Acts 8:12, "But when they believed Philip as he preached good news about the kingdom of God and the name of Jesus Christ, they were baptized, both men and women." The Pentecostal would say that having *believed* and having been *baptized*, they were Christians. Faith itself is a fruit of the Spirit (Gal. 5:22), an attribute of the divine nature, and is evidence of the Holy Spirit's activity in the interior life of the believer, even before the laying on of hands for the reception of the Holy Spirit for power-in-mission. In the case of the Samaritans, the charisms of the Spirit implied in the context are consistent with this view.

In terms of the conversion-initiation schema, however, it is claimed that "if they did not receive the Holy Spirit till later they cannot be called Christians until that time."[6] This judgment is reiterated in this added comment, "The mistake of many commentators is to assume that because the conditions of 2.38 had apparently been fulfilled, therefore, they were Christians and/or the Spirit had been given."[7]

Cutting through all the verbiage, the dichotomy between these respective viewpoints is the fundamental question at issue in the entire discussion.

Πιστεύειν **with a Dative Object**

The strategy of the conversion-initiation hypothesis here is to impugn the credibility of the Samaritans' faith. It is claimed, therefore, that "There are a number of reasons for believing not only that their response and commitment *was* defective, but also that Luke intended his readers to know this."[8] Of the reasons alleged to support this assumption, the following is, on the surface at least, the most conclusive one:

πιστεύειν also cannot bear the weight usually put on it. It is not here πιστεύειν εἰς; or ἐπὶ τὸν κύριον, but ἐπίστευσαν τῷ Φιλίππῳ; and when πιστεύειν governs a dative object (except perhaps κύριος or θεός) it signifies intellectual assent to a statement or proposition, rather than commitment to God (24.14; 26.27). This use of πιστεύειν, unique in Acts, can surely be no accident on Luke's part. He indicates thereby that the Samaritans' response was simply an assent of the mind to the acceptability of what Philip was saying and an acquiescence to the course of action he advocated, rather than that commitment distinctively described elsewhere which alone deserves the name 'Christian' (cf. John 2.23–25).[9]

The claim that "This use of πιστεύειν [is] unique in Acts" is beset with considerable ambiguity. In the same context with Acts 8:12 and 26:27, Bauer, Arndt, and Gingrich list examples from Matthew, Mark, Luke, and I John "w(ith) the per(son) to whom one *gives credence* or whom one *believes*, in the dat(ive)."[10] There are thirty or more instances of πιστεύειν with a dative object in some eleven books of the NT.[11] In what sense then that this idiom is unique to Acts is something less than clear. Nor is it explained how one may know when πιστεύειν with the dative object refers to intellectual assent, rather than commitment.

At the heart of the discussion is the tentative exclusion of κύριος and θεός from the rule as stated. This judgment is reversed, however, in a footnote, e.g., "Acts 5.14(?); 13.12(D); 16.34; 18.8 should also probably be given the sense of accepting the disclosures about rather than commitment to."[12] A significant omission from this list is Acts 27:25.

Before pursuing the discussion further, it is important to evaluate the disclaimer "(except κύριος and θεός)." On what grounds, one may ask, are these the exception to the rule, if a rule it be? There are certainly no grammatical or syntactical reasons for excepting them from the rule as stated. The sole excuse for their exclusion must be theological and not grammatical. But this is special pleading, and the reversal of this dictum in the footnote concedes as much.

On the other hand, if the texts are excluded in which κύριος and θεός form the dative object of πιστεύειν, the burden of proof favoring the claim that "it signifies intellectual assent rather than commitment to" rests with two texts, viz., Acts 24:14 and 26:27. Since Acts 8:12 is the text in question, it cannot be appealed to in order to establish the rule. Rather the rule must first be established before it can be applied to Acts 8:12 without the taint of special pleading.

On closer scrutiny of the first of these texts, Acts 24:14, a problem becomes immediately apparent. In nine texts in Acts in which the dative object occurs with πιστεύειν, eight are personal. In each instance, the response is to a person, not to a statement or proposition. Only in Acts 24:14 is it a dative of *the thing* to which one gives credence or believes, namely, τοῖς γεγραμένοις, "the things written," i.e., in the Law and the Prophets. Parallels to this idiom in John's Gospel challenge the claim to uniqueness in Acts. For example, "they believed the scripture and the word which Jesus had spoken (ἐπίστευσαν τῇ γραφῇ καὶ τῷ λόγῳ ὃν εἶπεν ὁ Ἰησοῦς)" (John 2:22; cf., 5:47). In the Johannine post-resurrection context, it cannot be contended that the disciples merely gave intellectual assent to the statements made earlier by Jesus. The claim for the uniqueness of the idiom in Acts is clearly special pleading. In any event, Acts 24:14 cannot be pressed on grammatical grounds to support any claim that Paul simply gave intellectual assent to the Law and the Prophets.

Thus, by a process of elimination of those passages cited in support of the conversion-initiation thesis, only one text remains, "King Agrippa, do you believe the prophets (τοῖς προφήταις)? I know that you believe" (Acts 26:27). Even though Agrippa's response was no more than an intellectual assent to the prophets, this does not prove that the Samaritans merely gave "an assent of the mind to the acceptability of what Philip was saying."[13]

Before this text can be claimed in support of this assumption, it must be shown that the *experience* of Agrippa was substantively commensurable with that of the Samaritans. But this has not been shown, nor can it be, for the following reason. Apostolic baptism involved a public confession of commitment to Jesus Christ. This is explicitly demonstrated by the exhortation of Ananias to Paul, "Rise and be baptized, and wash away your sins, *calling on his name*" (Acts 22:16).[14]

Furthermore, the authenticity of the Samaritans' baptism at the hands of Philip was acknowledged as authentic by Peter and John, for they did not rebaptize them before laying their hands upon them to receive the Holy Spirit. By way of contrast and illustration, it should be remembered that Paul rebaptized the Ephesian converts of John the Baptist before laying his hands upon them to receive the Spirit (Acts 19:5).

Unlike Agrippa, the Samaritans did more than give intellectual assent to Philip's message "about the kingdom of God and the name of Jesus Christ" (Acts 8:12). They believed and were baptized. The Samaritans believed in Jesus, and confessed His name in baptism. There is no hint in the context of Acts 26:27 that Agrippa either confessed faith in Christ, or was baptized—and therein a vast gulf is fixed between them. The example of Agrippa is not substantively commensurable with the experience of the Samaritans. Consequently, Acts 26:27 cannot be invoked to support the claim that the Samaritans gave only intellectual assent to the preaching of Philip.

Up to this point in our investigation, it may be argued that the evidence is at least inconclusive in favor of the assumption that "when πιστεύειν governs a dative object . . . it signifies intellectual assent to a statement or proposition, rather than commitment to God."[15] If the evidence to this point does not categorically refute the general assumption, it is at least sufficient to show that its application to Acts 8:12f. rests upon a very specious analogy.

If, on the other hand, as suggested in Dunn's footnote, those texts are to be included in which κύριος and θεός provide the dative object, the scope of the investigation is considerably broadened. The question that then confronts the conversion-initiation thesis is this. Can these texts really "be given the sense of accepting the disclosures about rather than commitment to?"[16]

The first in order of these texts is Acts 5:14(?), "And more than ever believers were added to the Lord." The reticence implied by "starring" this text with a question mark is justified. In the strictest sense τῷ κυρίῳ here is the object of προσετίθεντο, "believers *were added* to the Lord." They believed, and they were added to the Lord. Clearly these believers had given more than intellectual assent to the preaching of the apostles.

The faith of the proconsul on Cyprus who ἐπίστευσεν τῷ θεῷ ("believed in God") in Acts 13:12 (D) was contextually more than intellectual assent to the preaching of Paul and Barnabas. The whole point of the story is to record this first missionary triumph of the apostles.

In the context, Paul and Barnabas were summoned before the proconsul, Sergius Paulus, so that he might hear "the word of God" (v. 7). A Jewish magician and false prophet, Bar Jesus/Elymas by name, withstood them, and sought to turn the proconsul away from the faith (v. 8). Paul's denunciation of his interference resulted in the blindness of Elymas at the hand of the Lord (v. 11). The outcome of the conflict was the triumph of the gospel in the conversion of the proconsul (v. 12). If the proconsul had responded only with intellectual assent, it would have spelled the defeat of the apostles, but the story is told to record their double victory: first, in the defeat of a spiritual adversary and, second, in the conversion of the proconsul.

In the next citation, 16:34, the conversion of the Philippian jailer and his household, once again baptism implies confession of his newfound faith and suggests far more than intellectual assent, for, "Having believed in God (πεπιστευκὼς τῷ θεῷ)," he was baptized with his whole family (Acts 16:31, 34). The variant reading of this text, πεπιστευκὼς ἐπὶ τὸν θεόν (D), is an ancient witness to the fact that genuine commitment to God was involved.

Once again, Crispus, the ruler of the synagogue in Corinth, "believed in the Lord (ἐπίστευσεν τῷ κυρίῳ) together with his household" (Acts 18:8). Contextual consistency would require that these were among the "many of the Corinthians (who) hearing Paul believed and were baptized" (v. 8). Again faith in the Lord and baptism argue for full commitment to the Lord. As in the case of the Philippian jailer above, a textual variant, ἐπίστευσεν εἰς τὸν κύριον (D), favors the view that the faith of Crispus represented a real commitment to God. These variant readings, πεπιστευκὼς ἐπὶ τὸν θεόν (Acts 16:34) and ἐπίστευσεν εἰς τὸν κύριον (Acts 18:8), are, by Dunn's own admission, a convincing rebuttal to the thesis of the conversion-initiation paradigm.[17]

One last citation, Acts 27:25, omitted in the footnote referred to above, [18] is decisively against the argument from πιστεύειν with a dative object. The context is the storm at sea during Paul's journey to Rome. Seeking to reassure his fellow shipmates, he related to them the appearance of the angel to him and the words of assurance received from the angel that they should all survive the impending shipwreck. His recital closes with the affirmation, πιστεύω γὰρ τῷ θεῷ, "for I believe God." Paul's subsequent actions preclude any hint of merely intellectual assent to the message of the angel who appeared to him in the midst of the storm. The peril of the moment would argue against anything less than full acceptance of the divinely inspired word. The entire premise of the conversion-initiation hypothesis founders on Paul's unquestioned obedience to the angel's word. In matters of faith, Paul was no dilettante.

It may be concluded, therefore, that πιστεύειν with the dative object "cannot bear the weight [Dunn] puts on it." It is to be rejected as specious and arbitrary. The faith of the Samaritans was an authentic commitment to Jesus Christ.

Faith or Superstition (?)

Another reason given to account for the presumed defective faith and commitment of the Samaritans is that they "seem to have been a rather superstitious people."[19] Their superstitious response to Simon the sorcerer is regarded as indicative of a wave of mass eschatological emotion that gripped the whole area. It is considered significant that the Samaritan response to Philip is characterized by the same word (προσέχω), to "pay attention to what was said by Philip."[20]

This suggests that their reaction to Philip was for the same reasons and of the same quality and depth as their reaction to Simon (cf. vv. 6–8 with 10f.). It is hardly to be compared with Lydia's response to Paul's message (16.14), and the implication is that the Samaritans' acceptance of baptism was prompted more by the herd-instinct of a popular mass-movement (ὁμοθυμαδόν-v. 6) than by the self-and world-denying commitment which usually characterized Christian baptism in the early years.[21]

The comparison with Lydia is a tendentious one for which the text provides no justification. In the context, it is said that Lydia "was a worshipper of God" (16:14), i.e., a Jewish proselyte. The common elements in both accounts argue for parity rather than disparity in the response of both Lydia and the Samaritans. Lydia "gave heed" (προσέχεν) to what was said by Paul and was baptized. The Samaritans "gave heed" (προσεῖχον) to what was spoken by Philip, they believed and were baptized. The expression διήνοιξεν, "the Lord *opened* her heart," is simply a metaphorical way of saying that Lydia, like the Samaritans, believed and was baptized.

The attempt to set the Samaritans apart as an exceptional case—"a rather superstitious people"—is an excercise in special pleading. The practice of magic was a universal phenomenon in the ancient world at the dawn of the Christian Era. The Samaritans were no more superstitious than their Jewish neighbors, as contemporary sources clearly reveal. The *Aramaic Incantation Texts From Nippur* are a case in point.[22] These are a collection of Jewish magical texts from the Hellenistic period which show the pervasive nature of magic even among the Jews. The biblical text intimates as much, for among the itinerant Jewish exorcists in Ephesus were seven sons of a Jewish high priest, Sceva by name, who practiced exorcism with magical formulas (ἐξορκιστῶν).[23]

The allegations above raise another question. Was the response of the Samaritans the same in quality and depth as their former response to Simon? The text says that they believed, not simply in Philip, but "they believed Philip as he preached good news (ἐπίστευσαν τῷ φιλίππῳ εὐαγγελιζομένῳ) about the kingdom of God and the name of Jesus Christ." It was not simply a transfer of allegiance from Simon to Philip; it was a transfer of allegiance to Jesus Christ, the one whom Philip preached, for when the apostles at Jerusalem learned that "Samaria had *received the word of God*,"[24] they sent Peter and John to them (Acts 8:14).

The parallel with the response of the converts in Jerusalem on the day of Pentecost is not to be glossed over lightly by claiming that "The parallels between 8.5–13 and 2.41–47, and the miracles and joy present among the Samaritans (8.6–8) do not indicate that they already possessed the Spirit or were already converted."[25] But, that is precisely what the parallel does indicate. In response to Peter's preaching at Jerusalem, they received his word, they were baptized, and they were added to the Church—incidently without mention of the Holy Spirit until Acts 4:8, 31, and that in a nonconversion context. In Samaria they *received* (δέδεκται, *"approve[d], accept[ed]"*)[26] the word of God (8:14) from Philip and were baptized (8:12). The parallel with 2:41–47 argues that they were also added to the Church before Peter and John arrived in Samaria.

The additional appeal to the case of Simon as more or less normative for the interpretation of the Samaritans' response to Philip's preaching is an attempt to make the exception the rule. It is categorically alleged that

Luke makes it clear (vv. 12f.) that Simon's faith and baptism were precisely like those of the other Samaritans, as if to say, note carefully what I say, and do not miss the point: They all went through the form but did not experience the reality.[27]

The reasoning here rests upon a false analogy, for whatever else may be said of Simon, he cannot be the rule for the rest of the Samaritans. For instance, Judas was a disciple of whom Peter said, "For he was counted among us and received his portion in this ministry" (Acts 1:17). But, Judas's failure did not prejudice the integrity of the other apostles' commitment to Jesus. It is false logic to say that Simon's

falling away prejudices the integrity of the Samaritans' commitment to
the Lord.

A final word about Simon. Had he "not really fulfilled the conditions
for the gift of the Spirit (Acts 2.38) . . . (was he) a Christian in outward
form only, not in the NT sense of the word?"[28] The assumption is
supported by appealing to parallels from the OT and NT. The Septuagint version of Deut. 29:18–20 uses the same Greek words as Acts
8:23, "the gall of bitterness" (χολὴν πικρίας). Hebrews 12:15–17 is
cited as the other parallel. Conflating these two sources, the following
conclusion is drawn:

> He [Simon] was "doomed to taste the bitter fruit (χολὴν πικρίας) and wear the fetters of
> sin" (v. 23 NEB), for, like Esau (Heb. 12.15–17), he had a "root bearing poisonous and
> bitter fruit" (ἐν χολῇ καὶ ἐν πικρίᾳ) and therefore would know not the pardon but the
> anger of the Lord (Deut. 29.18–20).[29]

As noted already, the argument from analogy, even when—perhaps
one should say, especially when—supported by verbal correspon-
dences, must be applied cautiously and with due respect for the context.
It is fair to ask, then, if these parallels do support the conclusions drawn
from them. More specifically, do the verbal analogies sustain the conclusion that Simon was "a Christian in outward form only?"

In the context of Deut. 29:18–20, Moses warned the Israelites,
already in covenant relationship with Yahweh, "lest there shall be
among you a man or woman, or family or tribe, whose heart *turns away
today from the Lord our God*, to go and serve the gods of those
nations."[30] Although the word itself is not used in this text, clearly the
condition against which Moses warned them was apostasy, and apostasy is the abandonment of a previous loyalty. In the analogy drawn
from Esau, he could not sell "his own birthright," unless he truly
possessed it. Esau's judgment is the more severe because he spurned
what he already possessed. If then these analogies are to provide an
interpretative norm for Simon's experience, the conclusion they really
suggest is diametrically opposite to the above. Simon *was truly* a Christian who had apostatized. The text of Bezae preserves an interesting
variant that tends to support this conclusion. The text reads, "And
Simon answered, 'Pray for me to the Lord, that nothing of what you
have said may come upon me.'" To this the Bezan text adds, "who did
not stop weeping copiously (ὃς πολλὰ κλαίων οὐ διελίμπανεν)."[31]

The addition suggests tears of remorse, perhaps even of repentance.
Its very presence in the textual tradition of the NT ought to give one

pause before accepting at face value the assertion that Simon was "a Christian in outward form only."

Excursus on Acts 4:8, 31; 13:9

Inasmuch as Professor Dunn had singled out my views on Acts 4:8, 31, and 13:9 for rebuttal, a personal response is in order.

Ervin is the principal exception: he focuses attention on πίμπλημι as the key description of Spirit-baptism and argues that to be filled with the Spirit was a once-for-all experience. 4.31 he refers solely to the 3,000 converts of the day Pentecost, who did not receive the Spirit till then! 4.8 and 13.9 he refers back to Peter's and Paul's earlier Spirit-baptism (πλησθείς—who *had* been filled). 13.52 he takes to signify that the disciples ["converts." NEB] were filled one after another with joy and with the Holy Spirit (59–67, 71, 73). But while his interpretation of 13.52 is quite possible (cf. 8.18) his treatment of 4.31 involves some rather unnatural and tortuous exegesis which cannot be accepted. The "all" of 4.31 obviously includes the Christian community as a whole and Peter and John in particular—all in fact who took part in the prayer of 4.24–30. As for the formula πλησθεὶς πνεύματος ἁγίου εἶπεν, when an aorist participle is used with εἶπεν, it always describes an action or event which takes place immediately prior to or which leads into the act of speaking (e.g., Acts 1.15; 3.4; 5.19; 6.2; 9.17, 40; 10.34; 16.18; 18.6; 21.11). So with 4.8 it describes the sudden inspiration and empowering of the Spirit which Jesus had promised for the special occasion (Luke 12.11f: ἐν αὐτῇ τῇ ὥρᾳ) and which would not last beyond the hour of need. The same is probably true of 13.9. When Luke wants to indicate a lasting state of "fulness" resulting from a past "filling" the word he uses is πλήρης (Luke 4.1; Acts 6.3, 5, 8; 7.55).[32]

The problem here stems from radically different presuppositions, compounded by a failure to define terms clearly. In my understanding of the Pentecost narrative, the terms baptism in, filling with, and gift of the Holy Spirit are synonymous ways of describing the Pentecost event (Acts 1:8; 2:4, 33, 39; cf. Luke 24:49). Dunn's criticism of my position separates the *baptism in* from the *filling with* the Holy Spirit, but in my opinion it has not been demonstrated that subsequent uses in Acts of the expression "filling with the Spirit" are substantively distinct from those encountered in the Pentecost context. Baptism in the Holy Spirit (Acts 1:5) equals filled with the Holy Spirit (Acts 2:4). If, therefore, baptism in the Spirit is a once-and-for-all experience, and it is, then filling with the Spirit is a once-and-for-all experience also.

It is significant in this connection that Luke refers only twice to the Pentecostal experience as a baptism in the Spirit, Acts 1:5 and 11:16. Both are recorded as direct quotations of the words of Jesus. In every other reference to the Pentecostal experience, he uses a surrogate expression, e.g., "they were all filled with the Holy Spirit" (Acts 2:4;

4:31; 9:17); "they received the Holy Spirit" (Acts 8:17); "the gift of the Holy Spirit had been poured out even on the Gentiles" (Acts 10:44); "the Holy Spirit fell on the Eunuch" (Acts 8:39, Western text); "the Holy Spirit came on them" (Acts 19:6).

The first objection I would register is to the statement that "when an aorist participle [i.e., πλησθείς, Acts 4:8; 13:9] is used with εἶπεν, it always describes an action or event which takes place immediately prior to or which leads into the act of speaking." Even if the aorist participle is regarded as adverbial, it would simply designate an act prior to εἶπεν, but not necessarily *immediately* prior to the act of speaking.

The question at issue here, however, is this. Does Luke use the passive participle of a stative verb to "describe an action or event which leads into the act of speaking?" It is in part a question of syntax, the discussion of which will be deferred, for the moment. Suffice it to say here that the relation of πλησθείς to εἶπεν is bound up with the antecedent question of πλησθείς πνεύματος ἁγίου. Anticipating the subsequent discussion, an analogous idiom in Hebrew may be noted whereby "participles in connexion with genitives . . . are regarded as expressing a state."[33]

Pentecost marked the initial fulfillment of the promise of the Spirit for power-in-mission (Luke 24:49; Acts 1: 8ff.). In an earlier work, [34] I interpreted Acts 2:4, ἐπλήσθησαν πάντες πνεύματος ἁγίου, as an example of the ingressive aorist, which "is commonly employed with verbs which signify a state or condition, and denote entrance into that state or condition."[35] In Acts 2:5 the verb ἐπλήσθησαν (aorist, passive, 3rd person plural) is a finite form of the verb that views the action in its beginning. Pentecost marked the introduction of the disciples into the state of Spirit-fullness. The aorist passive participle, πλησθείς (Acts 4:8; 13:9), is not ingressive—after all, Pentecost marked the beginning of their experience with the fullness of the Spirit. It is, however, *stative*. It may also be regarded as a cumulative aorist that views the Pentecost event "from the viewpoint of its existing results."[36]

It is this stative sense of the aorist, passive participle, πλησθείς, that is at issue in Acts 4:8 and 13:9. This stative sense of the participle is caught in the translation, Good News for Modern Man, "Peter *full* of the Holy Spirit answered them."[37] Oddly enough, however, the same version fails of consistency in its translation of the parallel in Acts 13:9.

At issue also is a question of Luke's style in Acts. All of the participles with εἶπεν, cited by Dunn in support of his position, are active or middle voice rather than passive, and none are of stative verbs, e.g.: ἀναστάς, *stand up* (1:15); ἀτενίσας, *look intently* at (3:4); ἐξαγαγών, *bring out* (5:19); ἐπιθείς, *lay on*, of hands (9:17); ἐπιστρέψας, *turn* (9:40; 16:18); Ἀνοίξας, *open* (10:34); δήσας, *blind*, (21:11). The participles in Acts 6:2, προσκαλεσάμενοι, *summon*, and 18:6, ἐκτιναξάμενος, *shake out*, of clothes, are middle voice. All of these active and middle voice participles do "describe an action or event which leads into the act of speaking." I cannot agree, however, that the same dictum can be extended to the stative participle πλησθείς.

The stative sense is reinforced by the passive voice of πλησθείς. Voice and function are complementary. This is repeatedly illustrated in Luke's use of the verb πίμπλημι. It is used 24 times in the NT, 2 times in Matthew, and 22 times in Luke/Acts. It is used only twice in the active voice, once in Matt. 27:48, and once in Luke 5:7. On the other hand, Luke uses it 22 times in the passive voice. This indicatates that while the stative verb πίμπλημι may be used transitively in the active voice, under conditions dictated by the context—although from the textual evidence, these are more the exception than the rule—its use intransitively in the passive voice makes it unmistakably stative in function.

Furthermore, its disproportionate use in Luke/Acts, 22 times, as compared with Matthew's 2 times, marks its usage as distinctively Lukan. What is even more to the point, Luke/Acts uses the passive voice of πίμπλημι exclusively with states or conditions experienced by the subject of the verb; e.g.: πνεύματος ἁγίου, "the Holy Spirit" (Luke 1:15, 41, 67; Acts 2:4; 4:8, 31; 9:17; 13:9); ἡμέραι, "days" (Luke 1:23; 2:6, 21, 22; 21:22); χρόνος, "time" (Luke 1:57); θυμοῦ, "wrath" (Luke 4:28); φόβου, "fear" (Luke 5:26); ἀνοίας, "fury" (Luke 6:11); θάμβους καὶ ἐκστάσεως, "astonishment and amazement" (Acts 3:10); ζήλου, "jealousy" (Acts 5:17; 13:45); συγχύσεως, "*confusion*" (Acts 19:29).

The transitory nature of human emotions, however, does not argue for transitory and repeated fillings with the Holy Spirit. Parity between the categories of human emotions and Spirit-fullness cannot be demonstrated. Were this possible, then one could by the same logic argue that the new birth is also a transitory and repetitive experience.

As we shall see subsequently, the aorist passive participle, πλησθείς, sustains an adjectival relationship to the subject rather than an adverbial relationship to the verb εἶπεν. The single exception where πίμπλημι is used in the active voice (Luke 5:7, ἔπλησαν) is the exception that proves the rule. Luke's use of the aorist passive participle πλησθείς with εἶπεν cannot be construed as active in meaning, the sense necessitated by Dunn's interpretation.

The contrast with Luke's use of the cognate verb, πληρόω reinforces what has been said above. It is used 25 times in Luke/Acts. Luke uses the passive forms 13 times in both books and the active 11 times. In the Gospel of Luke the passive is used 7 times, the active 2 times. In Acts the ratio is reversed. The passive is used 6 times, and the active 9 times. If, therefore, Luke had *intended* to describe "the sudden inspiration and empowering of the Spirit," his distinctive uses of πίμπλημι and πληρόω would argue for the aorist *active* particle of πληρόω (i.e., πληρώσας) in Acts 4:8 and 13:9. The adverbial use of the plural form of the aorist active participle πληρώσαντες in Acts 12:25 reinforces this contention. It is also supported by the fact that all the aorist participles with εἶπεν cited by Dunn are active or middle rather than passive.

I conclude, therefore, that the use of the passive participle πλησθεὶς in Acts 4:8 and 13:9 describes an antecedent state or condition of Spirit fulness, not "an action or event immediately prior to . . . the act of speaking."

Two additional objections may be registered to the statement that "4.8 describes the sudden inspiration and empowering of the Spirit which Jesus had promised for the special occasion (Luke 12.11f.: ἐν αὐτῇ τῇ ὥρα) and which would not last beyond the hour of need."

1. The appeal to Luke 12:11f. is a category mistake. There is in it an implicit assumption that the sudden inspiration of the Spirit for the hour of crisis is synonymous with, and contingent upon, a renewed empowering of the Spirit, i.e., a new filling with the Spirit. The obvious objection to this assumption is that the text neither says, nor does it imply, that such is the case. From a theological point of view, the sudden inspiration of the Spirit in the face of imminent crises may just as well be attributed to the indwelling presence of the Spirit. The text in Luke says nothing about the sudden coming of the Spirit to match the sudden emergency. It says only that He is there in time of need. And consistent with Luke's use of the stative sense of πίμπλημι, the case for the abiding fullness of the Spirit is the more convincing one.

2. The claim that this inspiration and empowering "would not last beyond the hour of need" is at odds with the aorist tense of the participle in Acts 4:8 and 13:9. The assumption attributes a time factor to the aorist tense that is incompatible with the punctiliar sense of the aorist.

Professor Dunn is partly right—for an obvious reason—when he says that "When Luke wants to indicate a lasting state of 'fulness' resulting from a past 'filling' the word he uses is πλήρης." Πλήρης is a noun, cognate to the verb πληρόω, and nouns by their nature are statives. The concession that Luke does indicate that there *is* "a lasting state of 'fulness' resulting from a past 'filling,'" contradicts the contention that there are repeated "fillings" with the Spirit. After all, this is what I have argued for in reference to Acts 4:8 and 13:9.

A final word is in order about the syntax of the participles in the passages under scrutiny, specifically Acts 4:8. The clause reads, τότε Πέτρος πλησθεὶς πνεύματος ἁγίου εἶπεν πρὸς αὐτούς (then "Peter, full of the Holy Spirit, answered them").[38] The choice lies between the circumstantial and the attributive uses of the participle. However, the stative function of the participle argues against interpreting it as circumstantial, i.e., as adverbial qualifying the action of the verb εἶπεν. The stative function indicates that πλησθεὶς is used here as an anarthrous attributive, i.e., as an adjective without an accompanying article.

The attributive adjective stresses some quality or attribute of the noun it modifies. Freely translated, the clause reads, "the full-of-the-Spirit Peter said," which equals "Spirit-filled Peter said." Other illustrations of this syntactical relationship of the participle may be given. One more will suffice to illustrate it. Acts 22:3 reads in part, ἐγώ εἰμι ἀνὴρ Ἰουδαῖος, γεγεννημένος ἐν Ταρσῷ, "I am a man born-in-Tarsus, a Jew." This equals, "a Tarsus-born man, a Jew."[39] Thus, the adjectival use of the participle reinforces the stative sense of the passive participle in Acts 4:8 and 13:9.

In conclusion, I submit that the evidence adduced above supports my original contention that the baptism in/the filling with the Holy Spirit is a once-and-for-all experience resulting in a lasting fullness. Negatively, the evidence presented refutes the assertion that Act 4:8 "describes the sudden inspiration and empowering of the Spirit which Jesus had promised for the special occasion . . . and which would not last beyond the hour of need."[40] Inasmuch as the supportive evidence does confirm my thesis that the baptism in/filling with the Holy Spirit is a once-and-for-all experience, my interpretation of Acts 4:8, 31, 13:9 is not then an "unnatural and tortuous exegesis" but one thoroughly consistent with the immediate and the larger contexts of Acts.

Notes

[1] 1Dunn, op. cit., pp. 55–72.
[2] Ibid., p. 55.
[3] Inasmuch as I have been identified here in a footnote with the Pentecostal thesis, I must call attention to the fact that "chief stronghold" is a misrepresentation of my position. In a previous work, I pointed out, in some detail, that the Samaritan experience is one of seven contexts in Acts in which a "Pentecostal" pattern of conversion and

initiation with a subsequent baptism in/filling with the Holy Spirit for power-in-mission may be identified. Cf. *These Are Not Drunken As Ye Suppose* (Plainfield: Logos, [c] 1968), pp. 88–104.

[4]Dunn, op. cit., p. 55.

[5]Ibid., p. 39.

[6]Ibid., p. 55.

[7]Ibid., p. 68.

[8]Ibid., p. 63.

[9]Ibid., p. 65.

[10]Πιστεύω, 1., β., b.

[11]W. F. Moulton and A. S. Geden, *A Concordance to the Greek Testament* (1897; rpt. Edinburgh: T. & T. Clark, 1967).

[12]Dunn, op. cit., p. 65n.

[13]Ibid., p. 65.

[14]Italics added, cf. Acts 2:21; 9:14, 21; Rom. 10:13; I Cor. 1:2.

[15]Dunn, op. cit., p. 65.

[16]Ibid.

[17]Ibid., p. 64.

[18]Ibid., p. 65n.

[19]Ibid., p. 64.

[20]Bauer, Arndt, Gingrich.

[21]Dunn, op. cit., pp. 64, 65.

[22]James Alan Montgomery, *Aramaic Incantation Texts from Nippur* (Philadelphia: University Museum, 1913).

[23]Bauer, Arndt, Gingrich.

[24]Italics added.

[25]Dunn, op. cit., p. 57.

[26]Bauer, Arndt, Gingrich.

[27]Dunn, op. cit., p. 66.

[28]Ibid., p. 65.

[29]Ibid.

[30]NASB, italics added.

[31]Bruce Manning Metzger, *A Textual Commentary on the Greek New Testament* (New York: United Bible Societies, 1971).

[32]Dunn, op. cit., pp. 70, 71.

[33]*Gesenius' Hebrew Grammar*, ed. E. Kautzsch, 2nd English ed., A. E Cowley (Oxford: At the Clarendon Press, 1910).

[34]Howard M. Ervin, *These Are Not Drunken, As Ye Suppose* (Plainfield: Logos, [c] 1968).

[35]H. E. Dana and Julius R. Mantey *A Manual Grammar of the Greek New Testament* (New York: The Macmillan Co., 1955), p. 196.

[36]Ibid.

[37]Italics added.

[38]Good News For Modern Man.

[39]A. T. Robertson, *A Grammar of the Greek New Testament in the Light of Historical Research* (Nashville: Broadman Press, 1934), p. 1105. The use of the *perfect* passive participle in this illustration does not alter the parity of these examples. Tense does not affect state.

[40]Dunn, op. cit., p. 71.

Chapter 5

Paul's Conversion[1]

Was Paul converted at the time of his encounter with the risen Christ Jesus on the Damascus Road, or was his conversion "one single experience lasting from the Damascus road to the ministry of Ananias?"[2] Was he, at the time of Ananias's visit, already one of those who call upon the name of the Lord, or was he "not saved (2.21) until he ἐπικαλέσεται τὸ ὄνομα αὐτοῦ"[3] at his baptism (Acts 22:16)?

The Pentecostal replies that the use of the terms κύριε, "Lord," and ἀδελφός, "brother," indicates that Paul was converted by his encounter with the risen Jesus. Their case is simple, but not simplistic. Paul's conversion on the Damascus road was followed three days later by his filling with the Spirit through the laying on of Ananias's hands. However, in the logic of the conversion-initiation thesis, the view of Paul's conversion as instantaneous, followed by a subsequent filling with the Spirit, "is one which must be sharply questioned."[4] In the conversion-initiation polemic, "sharply questioned" translates as repudiated. The arguments in favor of the Pentecostal point of view that are to be thus "sharply questioned" are "principally that Paul called Jesus 'Lord' (9.5; cf. I Cor. 12.3), and that Ananias greeted him as 'brother' (9.17; 22.13)."[5]

Before discussing these two points, a clarification is in order. Pentecostals would agree that Paul was converted instantaneously—the phenomenon has parallels in every age of the Church; however, whether Paul made his commitment to Jesus at the precise moment that he addressed Him as κύριε, "Lord," does not in and of itself bear the full burden of proof for the Pentecostal understanding of the event. What is essential to the Pentecostal interpretation is the recognition that Paul had made such a commitment to Jesus *before* Ananias came to him, and addressed him as "brother Saul," meaning "brother Christian," in the sense that the title "Christian" is appropriate to the Church's self understanding at that time within a wholly Jewish ethos.

41

Κύριε, "Lord" or "Sir" (?)

To the first of these Pentecostal arguments, the following objection is offered, "in each case (9.5; 22.8, 10; 26.15) it is the vocative κύριε that Paul uses, and κύριε often means simply 'Sir'—a title of respect rather than a confession of faith."[6] But can it be assumed, without supporting evidence, that κύριε means no more than "Sir" in the context of Paul's experience? While the statement may seem plausible at first glance, it stops short of the full implications of the *experience*, as related by Paul. In recounting his Damascus-road experience in Acts 22:6ff., and 26:12ff., Paul added autobiographical details not recorded in Acts 9:1ff., and these details have a bearing upon his use of the title κύριε.

According to the account in Acts 22, Paul used the title twice, once before (22:8) and once *after* (22:10) Jesus' self-disclosure to him, "What shall I do, Lord" (κύριε, 22:10). The account in Acts 22:15ff. is more detailed and reflects the assumption that Paul's commitment was taken for granted. His words, "Wherefore, O King Agrippa, I was not disobedient to the heavenly vision," points to the theophanic context of the experience. When these three accounts of Paul's Damascus-road experience are combined, his commitment to Jesus is a natural assumption.

While it is true that the vocative κύριε *may* mean simply "Sir," the mere assertion of the fact does not prove that this is the meaning intended in Paul's salutation to the risen Christ in the Damascus-road encounter. Such a contention can be valid only when it is buttressed with contextual evidence, and apart from an allusion to Cornelius's experience, this has not been supplied. It is of the essence of the argument at this point to determine from a survey of the evidence when and under what circumstances Luke uses the vocative κύριε in the sense of "Sir."

In addition to Paul's use of the vocative κύριε in the context of the Damascus-road experience (Acts 9:5; 22:8, 10: 26:15), Luke uses it 11 more times in the book of Acts (i.e., 1:6, 24; 4:29; 7:59, 60; 9:10, 13; 10:14; 11:8; 22:19). In 10 of these passages, the meaning is unquestionably "Lord Jesus," rather than the noncommital, "Sir." Only in the eleventh instance is it applied to another than Jesus, and that to the "angel of God" who appeared to Cornelius in a vision (Acts 10:4). Only in this last example, where the subject addressed is another than Jesus, is it possible to suggest that the meaning may be "Sir," but even this is something more than dubious when it is understood in its context. Thus, the evidence strongly suggests that whenever Jesus is addressed as κύριε, the meaning is "Lord Jesus," and not the ambiguous "Sir."

Furthermore, when the context is consulted in which Cornelius used the vocative κύριε, a significant fact emerges. The one addressed is the "angel of God" who appeared to Cornelius in a *vision*, and the theophanic importance of such a vision in Acts is important in interpreting Luke's use of κύριε.

In the numinous-charged atmosphere of an angelic visitation, surely the vocative κύριε on the lips of Cornelius is pregnant with this sense of the Holy. One may legitimately question then whether the equivocal "Sir" is an appropriate expression of such numinous awe. When the subject of the theophany is Jesus himself, as in the Damascus-road theophany, the numinous quality of the encounter is increased immeasurably, as the preternatural phenomena accompanying the encounter indicate.

Theologically, the comparison of Paul's experience with that of Cornelius's—"like Cornelius, confronted by a glorious, majestic being, he [Paul] addresses him with awe, 'Sir,'"[7]—as qualitatively commensurable, is inappropriate on two counts. (1) The subject of Paul's vision was Jesus himself, and (2) the title "Sir"—appropriate when the subject addressed is another human being—is inadequate to express the reverential awe that the presence of deity might reasonably be expected to evoke. "Sir" may be sufficient to express the respect, deference, even the homage characteristic of liege and lord (lower case), but hardly the "awe" that predicates reverence before "a glorious, majestic being."[8] It is axiomatic, therefore, for the Pentecostal hermeneutic, that Paul's use of κύριε must be understood in the theological context of the accompanying theophany.

The importance of this theological context cannot be overstated, for the phenomenon occurs again and again in the Acts. Stephen, in the hour of his martyrdom, saw "the Son of man standing at the right hand of God" and cried, "Lord (κύριε) Jesus, receive my spirit" (Acts 7:56, 59). Ananias confronted by the Lord in a vision and hearing his summons, responded, "Here I am, Lord" (κύριε, Acts 9:10). Peter in an ecstasy saw the heavens opened and a great sheet full of animals descending, and he heard the voice of the Lord bidding him to "kill and eat." He replied, "No, Lord" (κύριε, Acts 10:14; 11:8). Upon Paul's return from Damascus, he experienced a second theophanic visitation from Jesus as he prayed in the temple. In it the Lord warned him to flee

Jerusalem for his life, and in responding to the warning, he once again addressed Jesus as "Lord" (κύριε, Acts 22:19).

Luke uses the vocative, κύριε, 15 times in Acts. It is used once in a question addressed to the risen Christ by His disciples prior to His ascension (Acts 1:6) and is used again by the apostles in a prayer for guidance in the selection of a successor to Judas (Acts 1:24). It appears 13 times in the context of theophanic visitations. Of the latter, Jesus is the subject in 12 of these instances. The cumulative effect of the evidence supports the view that Paul's use of κύριε, in the Damascus-road theophany means "Lord" and points to his commitment to Jesus then and there.

This raises another, related question. Was Paul's query, "Who are you Lord?" an expression of total ignorance of Jesus' identity, or was it in some sense rhetorical? Before the question is dismissed summarily as irrelevant, certain facts should be considered. Certainly Paul was cognizant of the disciples' claim that Jesus had been raised from the dead. Then, too, as "custodian" of the garments of those who stoned Stephen, Saul/Paul was a witness of his martyrdom. It is entirely plausible that Paul heard Stephen's cry, "Behold, I see the heavens opened, and the Son of man standing at the right hand of God" (Acts 7:56). It is equally plausible that he heard his prayer, "Lord (κύριε) Jesus, receive my spirit" (Acts 7:59). His last words must also have rung in Paul's ears, for he "cried with a loud voice, Lord (κύριε), do not hold this sin against them" (Acts 7:60).

The profound influence that this event had upon him is reflected in his later confession, "when the blood of Stephen thy witness was shed, I also was standing by and approving, and keeping the garments of those who killed him" (Acts 22:20). Perhaps, it is not strictly accurate to say that Paul's conversion was instantaneous. The narrative itself suggests that Paul's conversion, as distinguished from initiation, began with the martyrdom of Stephen and that the Damascus-road experience marked Paul's final capitulation to Jesus as Lord.

Of course, this is not meant to imply that Paul grasped the full significance of this supernatural visitation at once, but its implications for Paul's conversion were explicitly spelled out by the risen Christ, for He said to him, "I have appeared to you for this purpose, to appoint you to serve and bear witness to the things in which you have seen me and to those in which I will appear to you" (Acts 26:16). To the Pentecostal, therefore, it is special pleading to contend that Paul did not respond at that moment to Jesus' summons to discipleship.

A Psychological Explanation (?)

At this point in the discussion, the conversion-initiation hypothesis is buttressed by recourse to a pejorative psychological explanation of Paul's experience.

Rather, like Cornelius, confronted by a glorious, majestic being, he addresses him with awe, 'Sir' (10.4). It is hardly likely that the κύριε of 22.10 means more—scarcely credible, indeed, that the full implications of Jesus' reply should have been grasped by a dazed and shocked man and translated into full Christian commitment all in a matter of seconds.[9]

The hermeneutical importance of this presumed pathological effect upon Paul of the Damascus-road theophany is accentuated by the frequency of references to it. For example, it is claimed that

The blindness was obviously due, on the psychological level, to the sudden shock of being confronted with the glory of one whom he thought of as a blasphemer and law-breaker justly done to death.[10]

This preoccupation with the psychological explanation leaves unasked the question of physiological causes related to Paul's blindness. The fact that the light was seen not only by Paul but also by his entourage attests to its objective character (Acts 22:9). It is appropriate to ask what effect such a brilliant flash of light might have upon the retina or the optic nerves of one in direct line of sight. But what is even more important for the interpretation of the event is the insensitivity of the psychological explanation to the theological context, for the whole question is related to the "uncreated light" in the mystical experience of saints and sages in the whole economy of redemption.

In the explanation of Paul's three-day fast after his encounter with Jesus on the Damascus road, several commentators are quoted in support of the statement that

His neither eating nor drinking during the next three days (9.9) is best explained as a consequence and symptom of a state of shock. . . . It is well known that serious mental shocks often have physical consequences.[11]

This explanation reflects a further insensitivity to the importance of fasting-prayer as a spiritual discipline. But then neither mystical theology nor spiritual exercises figure in the psychological explanation offered above.

From the foregoing premises it is concluded that

When we realize how this encounter with Jesus cut to the very roots of Paul's personality and worldview it becomes impossible to think [i.e., psychologically or theologically (?)] that he was converted in an instant.''[12]

Whatever psychological insights may contribute to the interpretation of the event, it cannot be at the expense of the theological context. From the standpoint of the biblical theologian, the psychological explanation offered above misses completely the theological import of the event.

Certainly, there is no biblical warrant for presuming that the theophany produced a pathological emotional state in Paul with concomitant hysteric manifestations, e.g., blindness and involuntary fasting. As a matter of record, the biblical theophanies are notable for their life-changing power. The word of Yahweh came to Abraham in a theophany (Gen. 18:1ff.) and altered redemptively not only his worldview but that of subsequent generations of the faithful. Yahweh appeared to Moses in the midst of a burning bush (Ex. 3:1ff.) and summoned him to be the deliverer of his people from Egyptian bondage. The experience not only altered his personality (from fugitive murderer to deliverer) and worldview, it altered the subsequent course of history. Isaiah's call-vision in the temple was a theophany of the Lord ('*Adonai* = κύριε, Isa. 6:1ff.), and it changed dramatically his personality and worldview. He became both prophet and statesman whose words sustained Judah in the midst of national crises and helped to lay the foundation for a renewed remnant.

In none of these encounters with the Lord are pathological or hysteric symptoms indicated. Nor are abnormal symptoms discernible in any of the theophanies already noted in the book of Acts. Consequently, it cannot be too strongly emphasized that the biblical theophanies—including the encounter on the Damascus road—cannot be explained (or explained away) in terms of pathological emotional states. Rather, their most noteworthy consequence for the history of redemption is their power to transform the lives of individuals and, through them, of society itself.

'Αδελφός: **"Fellow Jew" or "Fellow Christian" (?)**

The evidence surveyed thus far favors the Pentecostal view that Paul was converted during his encounter with Jesus on the Damascus road. Consequently, when Ananias addressed him as "Brother" (Acts 9:17;

22:13), he acknowledged a spiritual kinship with Paul as "fellow Christian" rather than a common national identity, "fellow Jew." On the other hand, it is essential to the conversion-initiation thesis that Ananias's salutation means nothing more than "fellow Jew."

Once again, the methodological approach is a curious one in the light of the previous discussion of κύριε. No comprehensive exegesis was offered there beyond the simple assertion that it "often means simply 'Sir.'" In the present instance, however, a statistical enumeration of the uses of ἀδελφός, *brother*, in Acts is resorted to as supportive of the conversion-initiation hypothesis. It must be pointed out that statistical probability is not a substitute for contextual exegesis. It cannot arbitrate the meaning of a word in a specific context. The final meaning of the word in question always rests with a critical, contextual exegesis of the passage.

The evidence in favor of the conversion-initiation paradigm is summarized thus:

ἀδελφός is used 57 times [*sic*] in Acts—33 times equivalent to "my fellow Christian(s)" (leaving aside 9.17 and 22.13), and 19 times in reference to the national/spiritual kinship of Jew to Jew. [If the purpose here is to establish by a statistical probability the meaning of ἀδελφός in Acts 9:17 and 22:13, then the arithmetic favors the meaning "fellow Christian."] . . . and in the 18 cases where ἀδελφός is used in the vocative (as here), 13 mean fellow Jews and only 5 = 'fellow Christians'.[13]

It is clear from this last statement that it is the use of ἀδελφός in the vocative that is essential to the argument and not the statistical count.

Thus, while Dunn has been content to rest his case on a statistical count of the uses of ἀδελφός in the vocative, he has apparently seen nothing significant in the contextual uses of the vocative, again a curious oversight. For instance, all of the uses of the vocative of ἀδελφός in Acts are plural except 9:17; 21:20 and 22:13, and two of these (9:17 and 22:13) are the passages in dispute. Significantly, all of these instances of the singular vocative refer to Paul. In every example in which the plural is used, and one in which the singular is used (Acts 21:20), the context makes it clear whether the reference is to their national identity as Jews or to their spiritual kinship as believer in Jesus as the Messiah.

So the fundamental question at issue remains unanswered by simply tabulating the uses of ἀδελφός in Acts. What it has done is to sharpen the question: What does the singular vocative, ἀδελφέ, mean when addressed to Paul?

Of the three passages where the singular vocative is addressed to

Paul, the context of Acts 21:20 makes it plain that it means "brother Christian." James and the elders of the Jerusalem church having heard the recital of Paul's missionary labors among the Gentiles, responded, "You see, brother (ἀδελφέ), how many thousands there are among the Jews of those who believed." Unquestionably, the singular vocative addressed to Paul here means "fellow Christian." While the evidence of this passage is, of course, not conclusive for the interpretation of the vocative in 9:17 and 22:13, it is presumptive evidence that Luke's use of the vocative when addressed to Paul means "fellow Christian." Lacking clear-cut contextual evidence to the contrary, it is difficult to deny the force of this assumption, especially since it is consistent with two other, convergent lines of evidence already discussed.

1. The theophanic context of the Damascus-road event is important. Ananias's natural fear of Saul/Paul as the persecutor of the Christians required divine assurance of the change in Paul before he ventured to go to him.

2. The words of divine reassurance of Paul's "chosenness"—"Go, for he is a chosen instrument of mine" (Acts 9:15)—would naturally predispose him to receive Paul as one already sharing a common commitment to Jesus.

The foregoing discussion vindicates the Pentecostal understanding that Paul's conversion was instantaneous and that he was subsequently "filled with the the Holy Spirit" (Acts 9:17) when Ananias laid his hands upon him. Conversely, it may be said that the "sharp questioning" to which the Pentecostal position was subjected has not impugned its credibility. Rather, an analysis of the conversion-initiation arguments has demonstrated serious methodological weaknesses in them.

A Normative Pattern

A parting shot cannot pass unnoticed. It is asserted that

Luke's failure to relate Paul's actual reception of the Spirit makes it impossible to decide finally whether it happened at the laying on of Ananias's hands (9.17; cf. 8.17; 19.6) or at his baptism (9.18; cf. 22.6). 9.17 cannot therefore be used as positive evidence for the relationship either between Spirit-baptism and water-baptism, or between the gift of the Spirit and the laying on of hands.[14]

The ambiguity (?) that gives Dunn pause here is not in the biblical text itself, but in the conversion-initiation syllogism. There is in fact a twofold rationale for the relationship between the gift of the Spirit and the laying on of hands. In the first place, the baptism in the Spirit in Acts is not presented as conversion-initiation but as empowerment-for-mission. Secondly, the recognition that there is discernible a normative pattern in the Spirit's activity in Acts dissolves the uncertainty into one of sound rather than substance. For example, after the statement regarding the eunuch's baptism, the Western text preserves a provocative variant (Acts 8:39), "The Spirit of the Lord fell upon the eunuch, and an angel of the Lord snatched away Philip." Henry Alford suggested that the variant probably arose "from a desire to conform the results of the eunuch's baptism to the usual method of the divine procedure."[15]

The "usual method of the divine procedure" was repentance, faith, baptism, and then the baptism in the Holy Spirit for power-in-mission to the world. Thus, conversion and inititation "normally" precede Spirit-baptism. Insofar as this normative pattern applies to the laying on of hands for the reception of the Spirit, it is discernible in the "Samaritan Pentecost" in which Peter and John "laid their hands on them and they received the Holy Spirit" (Acts 8:17).

In the light of the assertion that "9.17f. cannot therefore be used as positive evidence for the relationship . . . between the gift of the Spirit and the laying on of hands," it is appropriate to call attention to the fact that "when Paul laid his hands upon them [the Ephesian converts] the Holy Spirit came on them" (Acts 19:6). These categorical affirmations, linking the reception of the Spirit to the laying on of hands, make it difficult to comprehend Dunn's ambivalence apart from a priori theological assumptions.

Such a normative pattern of the Spirit's activity justifies the conclusion that Paul himself received the Holy Spirit when Ananias laid his hands upon him. In the context, surely this is the most natural understanding of Ananias's words to Paul, "Brother Saul, the Lord Jesus . . . has sent me that you may regain your sight, and be filled with the Holy Spirit" (Acts 9:17).

As for Paul's water baptism occurring after his reception of the Spirit, perhaps the most that needs to be said for inverting the normal conversion and initiation sequence (repentance, faith, and water baptism) is that, in the case of a "chosen instrument," God is not bound by precedent. The experience of Cornelius and his household would imply that God is never bound by precedent. One is, however, reminded of Paul's own claim that God "had set me apart before I was born" (Gal. 1:15). The exception simply proves that there is a rule, or normative pattern; otherwise, the exception itself becomes the rule.

Notes

[1]Cf. Dunn, op. cit., pp. 73–82.
[2]Ibid., p. 77.
[3]Ibid., p. 75.
[4]Ibid., p. 73.
[5]Ibid.
[6]Ibid.
[7]Ibid., p. 74.

[8]John's reaction to the encounter with just such "a glorious, majestic being" in his Patmos vision is another case in point: "I John am the one who heard and saw these things. And when I heard and saw, I fell down *to worship* at the feet of the angel who showed me these things" (Rev. 22:8; NASB, italics added).

[9]Dunn, op. cit., p. 74.
[10]Ibid., p. 75.
[11]Ibid.
[12]Ibid., pp. 75, 76.
[13]Ibid., p. 74.
[14]Ibid., p. 78.
[15]*The Greek Testament*, II (Cambridge: Deighton, Bell and Co., 1865), p. 96.

Chapter 6

Cornelius's Conversion

The discussion of "The Conversion of Cornelius"[1] begins with the customary anti-Pentecostal rhetoric, "With Acts 10 the Pentecostal is in difficulty from the start: There appears to be no grasp between the conversion of Cornelius and his Spirit-baptism."[2] If the Pentecostal is understandably puzzled by this accusation, it is because in his *grasp* of conversion and Spirit-baptism these are clearly distinguishable and sequential acts of the Holy Spirit.

The alternative offered by the conversion-initiation thesis is conveniently summarized thus:

> 11.14–18 concentrates exclusively on God's acceptance of Cornelius; Cornelius was saved, was baptized in the Spirit, was given the Spirit, was granted repentance unto life—all synonymous ways of saying: Cornelius became a Christian. The baptism in the Spirit therefore was not the consequence of a further step of faith on Cornelius's part, for he knew only of belief unto salvation; but when he thus believed he received the saving, life-giving baptism in the Spirit.[3]

The Pentecostal must perforce object to the conflating of these clearly distinguishable and normally sequential facets of conversion and initiation with the baptism in the Spirit for power-in-mission under the rubric "synonymous ways of saying: Cornelius became a Christian."

The expression, "you shall be baptized in the Holy Spirit," occurs twice in Acts. It is used first in Acts 1:5 and again in the context under discussion, Acts 11:16. In both instances Luke records them as direct quotations of the words of Jesus. It is most important for the interpretation of Cornelius's experience to note the context in which these quotations are set.

This text is part of Peter's self-vindication in the face of the charges of "the circumcision party" in the church at Jerusalem, i.e., the Judaizers (11:2). The charge itself had to do with Peter's violation of the Jewish dietary laws, to the observant Jew, a serious charge indeed. In the words of his accusers, "Why did you go to uncircumcised men and eat with them?" So serious was this charge that only Peter's appeal to a divine intervention, such as they themselves had experienced at Pentecost, could exonerate him in the eyes of his "orthodox" accusers.

Peter concluded his defense with these words, "As I began to speak, the Holy Spirit fell on them just as on us at the beginning. And I remembered the word of the Lord how he said, 'John baptized with water, but you shall be baptized with the Holy Spirit.'" The words, "the Holy Spirit fell on them *just as on us at the beginning*," are crucial for interpreting Cornelius's experience.[4] It is clear from these words that the baptism in the Spirit of Cornelius and his household is identified by Peter as *qualitatively* the same baptism in the Spirit received by the apostolic community on the day of Pentecost. If there were any doubt of this, Peter dispells it by adding that God gave to Cornelius and his household "*the same* (ἴσην) gift as *He gave* to us also after believing in the Lord Jesus Christ" (Acts 11:17).[5]

Thus the words of Peter, "at the beginning" and "the same gift," are normative for the understanding of Cornelius's baptism in the Spirit. The interpretation of the Pentecostal effusion of the Spirit is thus the *interpretative norm* for understanding the Spirit-baptism of the Roman centurion. Thus, one's interpretation of Pentecost will determine one's understanding of Cornelius's experience. One thing the Pentecostal will say categorically. The baptism in the Spirit of the Church on the day of Pentecost was *not* "the saving, life-giving baptism in the Spirit."

From the Paschal insufflation of the Spirit (John 20:22), the apostolic community *was* the Church, in the full sense of the word, before the Holy Spirit came *upon* them conferring power to witness (with signs following) "in Jerusalem, and in all Judea and Samaria, and even to the remotest part of the earth" (Acts 1:8). By parity of reasoning then, the baptism in the Spirit of the Roman household was *qualitatively* the same baptism in the Spirit experienced by the apostolic community in Jerusalem on the day of Pentecost. In both instances, it was enduement for power-in-mission, not "the saving, life-giving baptism in the Spirit" postulated in the conversion-initiation hypothesis.

Acts 15:8 is claimed by the conversion-initiation schema as confirmation of its assertions. It is a Pentecostal perception, however, that on closer examination, the passage favors the Pentecostal position, e.g., "God who knows the heart [of the Gentiles to whom 'he granted repentance unto life,' (11:18)] bore witness to them, giving them the Holy Spirit just as he did to us" (Acts 15:8). The gift of the Holy Spirit to Cornelius and his household was God's witness to their qualifications for admission to the Church by faith apart from circumcision. Faith was present before the communication of Spirit, and it was by this faith that God cleansed their hearts (Acts 15:9). Thus, the gift of the Holy Spirit, manifested in the charism of tongues, was God's witness to the saving grace already received through faith.

Conversion and the regenerating action of the Holy Spirit are preconditions for receiving the power of the Spirit through Spirit-baptism. As in the case of the apostolic community, these may be separated by fifty days (Passover to Pentecost), or by an indefinite period of time as in the Samaritan "Pentecost," or by three days in Paul's Damascus-road experience, or as in the present instance in close proximity to each other. In each instance, either explicitly or implicitly, the baptism in the Spirit is accompanied by a unique manifestation of the Holy Spirit's presence, viz., speaking in tongues.

This raises a question that the Pentecostal would address to the protagonist of the conversion-initiation thesis. If the baptism in the Spirit is simply subsumed as an episode in conversion-initiation, what role does "speaking in tongues" play in conversion-initiation? In the experiences in Jerusalem and Caesarea they were not incidental to the reception of the Spirit. It was in fact the "sign" (Mark 16:17; I Cor. 14:22) of tongues that convinced the Jewish disciples who accompanied Peter that Cornelius and his household had received the Spirit.

If then speaking in tongues is the *sign* that validates the baptism in the promised Holy Spirit in Jerusalem, Caesarea, and Ephesus, (implicitly in Damascus and Samaria), can the gift of the Spirit be separated exegetically from the *sign*? Anticipating a rejoinder, the Pentecostal must insist that a dispensational divide cannot be invoked to negate the exegesis of the text. The terms of the promised baptism in the Spirit have not been altered dispensationally. Peter, expounding to an astonished multitude the phenomenon of the Spirit's coming at Pentecost, said, "For the promise [the baptism in the Spirit] is to you [those listening to Peter's words] and to your children [their descendants] and to all that are far off [the Gentiles], every one whom the Lord our God calls to himself" (Acts 2:39). If God is still "calling to himself," and he is, then *the promise* (the baptism in the Holy Spirit) is still in effect. And there is no exegetical evidence that would support expunging the charisms of the Spirit from this paradigm. The conversion-initiation hypothesis is faced with a predicament that allows for only two choices. Either separate the baptism in the Spirit (for power-in-mission) from the conversion-initiation schema, or else acknowledge that conversion-initiation is incomplete until the convert speaks with tongues, "as the Spirit gives utterance."

In a Pentecostal understanding of the experience of the apostles, two distinct works of the Spirit are identified, namely, at Passover and again at Pentecost. In the former, Jesus appeared to His diciples on the evening of the resurrection day, and He "breathed (ἐνεφύσησεν) on them, and said to them, 'Receive the Holy Spirit'" (John 20:22). In our opinion, this is neither a "Johannine Pentecost," nor is it to be understood proleptically of their subsequent baptism in the Spirit at Pentecost. Rather, as God breathed the breath of life (ἐνεφύσησεν, Gen. 2:7)[6] into Adam on the day of the first creation, so too the risen Christ breathed spiritual life into His disciples on the resurrection day, the day of the new creation.

The Pentecostal baptism in the Spirit was designed to launch the Church upon its agelong, worldwide mission of evangelism, with signs following confirming the word that the apostles preached. Inasmuch as Peter appealed to Pentecost as the analogue for interpreting Cornelius's Spirit-baptism, then by parity of reasoning, the Roman "Pentecost" was neither "saving" nor "life-giving" (as Dunn asserts), but empowerment for mission.

Notes

[1]Dunn, op. cit., pp. 79–82.

[2]Ibid., p. 79.

[3]Ibid., p. 81. Whatever views others may hold, it is not my understanding that the baptism in the Spirit "was a consequence of a further step of faith on Cornelius's part." It is rather a subsequent action of the Holy Spirit consequent upon his regenerating action.

[4]Italics added.

[5]NASB, italics added.

[6]Septuagint.

Chapter 7

The Ephesian "Disciples"

Who were the twelve disciples that Paul met at Ephesus (Acts 19:1–7)? The interpretation of their experience is bound up with the answer to this question. In the discussion of "The 'Disciples' at Ephesus,"[1] "three major strands" in a strong Pentecostal case are identified for rebuttal.

(a) The twelve Ephesians were Christians (μαθηταί, οἱ πιστεύσαντες) before Paul met them—Christians, that is who had not received the Holy Spirit.

(b) Paul's question in 19.2 seems to imply that for Paul one could be a Christian yet not have (received) the Spirit. [a and b are closely related].

(c) The time interval between the Ephesians' baptism and Paul's laying on of hands means that there was a time interval between conversion (which precedes baptism) and the coming of the Spirit (which followed the laying on of hands).[2]

The nuancing of the first of these *strands* is misleading. No responsible Pentecostal theologian would argue *simpliciter* that they were Christians who had not received the Holy Spirit. Implicit in the Pentecostal position is the understanding that, if they were Christians, then they had experienced the regenerating work of the Holy Spirit through repentance and faith but had not been baptized in the Spirit for power-in-mission.

As a counter to this first strand, it is claimed that "they are disciples, but do not yet belong to *the* disciples; that is, they are not yet Christians."[3] This conclusion is supported by an exegesis of μαθηταί, *disciples*.

It is true that in Acts μαθηταί usually equals "Christians," but the 19.1 usage is unique: it is the *only* time that μαθηταί is not preceded by the definite article. Now οἱ μαθηταί used absolutely always has the sense in Acts of the *whole* Christian community of the city or area referred to, not just "Christians" generally, but the whole body of disciples as a single entity.[4]

The point made here is that μαθηταί with *the definite article*, οἱ, identifies the aggregate of the disciples in a given locality as the church in that place. Hence the absence of the definite article with μαθηταί in Acts 19:1 is proof (?) that the Ephesian "disciples" did not belong to what is referred to as "the church at Ephesus."[5] Confirmation for this is found in the additional observation that "Luke's description of the twelve as τινες μαθηταί therefore probably implies that the twelve did *not* belong to 'the disciples' in Ephesus—a fact confirmed by their ignorance of basic Christian matters."[6]

At first glance, the argument based on a distinction (real or fancied) between οἱ μαθηταί and τινες μαθηταί , may seem plausible, but on closer scrutiny, its logic is seriously flawed by its methodology. This may be illustrated by arranging the argument in the form of a syllogism.

Major premise: in Acts οἱ μαθηταί is used to designate "the whole Christian community of the city or area referred to . . . as a single entity."

Minor premise: The Ephesian disciples are referred to as τιυες μαθηταί rather than οἱ μαθηταί.

Conclusion: Therefore, the Ephesian disciples did not belong to the Christian community in Ephesus.

While the conclusion itself is too facile, the primary focus of our inquiry at the moment is not the conclusion, but the methodology. It leaves unanswered, because unasked, some important questions. (1) Is there contextual evidence for a body of disciples in Ephesus, at that time (19:1), called οἱ μαθηταὶ ἐν Ἐφέσῳ? (2) Is τινες μαθηταί a valid criterion for determining the relation of the Ephesian disciples to the Christian community?

First of all, is there contextual evidence for a body of disciples in Ephesus, at that time (19:1), called οἱ μαθηταὶ ἐν Ἐφέσῳ? The reader is informed that there is a Christian community referred to as "οἱ μαθηταὶ ἐν Ἰερουσαλήμ (6.7); οἱ ἐν Δαμασκῷ μαθηταὶ (9.19); οἱ μαθηταὶ [ἐν *(sic)* Ἰόππῃ] (9.38); οἱ μαθηταὶ ἀπὸ Καισαρείας (21.16)."[7] The reader is *not* informed, however, that there is *no* Christian community in Ephesus (19.1) referred to as οἱ μαθηταὶ ἐν Ἐφέσῳ until three months *after* Paul's return to Ephesus on his third missionary journey (19:9, τοὺς μαθητάς). Individual disciples? Yes! Priscilla and Aquila, for example, were there. A "whole body of disciples as a single entity?"—the reference to "the brethren" (οἱ ἀδελφοὶ, 18:27) may be an allusion to such, but, if this is so, they are still identified with the synagogue. Since there are, in the context, no οἱ μαθηταὶ prior to Acts 19:9, the logic of Dunn's argument would exclude them, as well as Apollos, from a Christian community in Ephesus. However, in the fluid state of the Christian witness prior to Paul's return (19:1), such terms as οἱ μαθηταί and τινες μαθηταί cannot be absolutized in favor of the conversion-initiation hermeneutics. A brief digression will set this in focus.

At the close of Paul's second missionary journey, he stopped briefly at Ephesus on his way to Antioch (18:19). The only record of his missionary labors during his first visit is compressed into one brief notice, "And they came to Ephesus, and he left them there [i.e., Priscilla and Aquila]; but he himself went into the synagogue and argued with the Jews" (18:19). His reception was cordial enough for them to press him to stay longer. He declined with the promise that in the providence of God he would return (18:19–21). The fact that no church is mentioned there and that the synagogue was the focus of Paul's activities supports the hypothesis that *the church as a distinct entity* had not yet been established at Ephesus. An implicit contrast between synagogue and church is indicated in the sequel, for setting sail from Ephesus and arriving at Caesarea, "he went up and greeted the church" (18:22), before going on to Antioch. From the synagogue in Ephesus (18:19) to the church in Caesarea (18:22)—the contrast is clearly defined.

When Paul returned to Ephesus on his third journey, the synagogue was still the focus of his endeavors (19:8). This continued for three months (19:8), until faced with the opposition and vilification of his adversaries in the synagogue, "he withdrew from them, taking the disciples (τοὺς μαθητάς) with him, and argued daily in the hall of Tryannus" (19:9). *Only then* are the disciples referred to collectively as τοὺς μαθητάς—"the whole Christian community of the city." Thus the contrast between οἱ μαθηταί, *the* disciples who are the church in Ephesus, and τινες μαθηταί, *some* disciples who are not the church in Ephesus, is shown to be without convincing contextual support. How can the disciples of Acts 19:1 be compared with "the *whole* Christian community of the city," when the Christian community was indistinguishable from the synagogue?

The self-contradictory nature of the argument is compounded by the further claim that although "the twelve did *not* belong to 'the disciples' in Ephesus," nevertheless, "we may not simply dub them 'disciples of John the Baptist'; the use of μαθηταί requires some connection with Christianity, and presumably Paul must have had some reason for addressing them as οἱ πιστεύσαντες."[8] These claims are paradoxical, to say the least. The contradiction is compounded by the last statement, for just eight lines above, it was said, "Nor need the πιστεύσαντες mean any more than a mistaken (or charitable) presumption on Paul's part."[9]

The argument is overly subtle, for the obvious implications of the context are that the disciples of Acts 19:1ff. were disciples of John the Baptist. The fact of their rebaptism is in itself a value judgment on the incompleteness of John's baptism of repentance. Although it was a baptism in preparation for the imminent coming of the messianic age, the context makes it clear that they were ignorant of the identity of the Messiah who had already come. Paul's words bear witness to this, for he said to them, "John baptized with the baptism of repentance, telling the people to believe in the one who was to come after him, that is Jesus" (Acts 19:4). It was after they heard this that "they were baptized in the name of the Lord Jesus" (19:5). They had experienced John's baptism, but it remained for Paul to relate to them the personal history of Jesus as the One to whom John had directed their faith. They were disciples of John, and in that sense disciples of the messianic age, needing only to know the identity of the One whose coming their faith anticipated. A reading of the context makes it clear that a contrast is intended between John's baptism as preparatory, and baptism "in the name of the Lord Jesus," the latter completing what was initiated in the former. Otherwise why place them in such obvious juxtaposition?

However, from the Pentecostal point of view, the question is not so much their status when Paul met them, as it is their status *after* they were baptized and *before* Paul laid his hands upon them to receive the Holy Spirit. Faith in Jesus and water baptism are preconditions for the laying on of hands to receive the Holy Spirit *with* the special charisms of tongues and prophesying (19:6).

We address now the second question raised above. Is τινες μαθηταί a valid criterion for determing the relation of the Ephesian disciples to the Christian community? The fundamental question that must be addressed is simply this. Does the indefinite pronoun, τινες, imply a contrast with the definite article οἱ? Does the use of the indefinite pronoun, in and of itself, exclude these disciples from the whole Christian community? The question must be examined in the larger context of Acts.

Does the use of the indefinite pronoun in other contexts exclude disciples from other Christian communities? Conversely, it may be asked if Luke uses the indefinite pronoun to identify disciples who are fully Christian in other geographical areas? If this is so, it may then be argued that the indefinite pronoun in Acts 19:1 neither includes nor excludes the Ephesian disciples from the Christian community. It simply says that they are disciples—of whom, or of what, must be derived from other factors in the context. The contrast between the whole, οἱ, and the part, τινες, is therefore irrelevant to their identity.

The claim that "the 19.1 usage is unique" is, as already shown, blemished by the circumstantial nature of the supporting evidence. Does Luke, on the other hand, use the indefinite pronoun to identify other disciples individually without reference to their local community? The answer is, of course, yes, and three separate passages in Acts bear this out.

1. Acts 9:10, "Now there was a certain disciple (τις μαθητὴς) at Damascus, named Ananias."[10]

2. Acts 9:36, "Now in Joppa there was a certain disciple (τις ἦν μαθήτρια) named Tabitha."

3. Acts 16:1, "And behold, a certain disciple (μαθητής τις) was there, named Timothy."

In these examples the indefinite pronoun is used to designate individual Christians without reference to the Christian communities with which they were identified. To be more specific, there is in these examples no contrast expressed or implied between οἱ μαθηταί and τις μαθητής. This is all the more trenchant a rebuttal of Dunn's argument inasmuch as the reader has already been informed that there was a οἱ ἐν Δαμασκῷ (where Ananias resided), and a οἱ μαθηταί [ἐν Ἰόππῃ] (where Tabitha lived).

The fact that the singular indefinite pronoun is used in these examples, while the plural is used in Acts 19:1, does not alter the point at issue. The point to be understood is simply that the use of the indefinite pronoun either of individuals (Acts 9:10, 36; 16:1) or of a group (Acts 19:1) is insufficient grounds for assuming that they are not a part of the Christian community in a given area or locality. Nothing more is intended by these remarks. Our concern has been to expose the inadequacy of both the methodology and the criteria used to support the conversion-initiation argument.

Excursus on Apollos

The remark noted earlier that "the twelve did *not* belong to 'the disciples' in Ephesus—a fact confirmed by their ignorance of basic Christian matters,"[11] is analogous to the case of Apollos. Contextually, their ignorance of "basic Christian matters" concerned matters of baptism, i.e., water-baptism, "in the name of the Lord Jesus" (19:5) and Spirit-baptism (19:2). It is, however, something of an enigma that, as disciples of John, they were apparently unaware of the promised messianic baptism in the Spirit, and no explanation is offered in the context. Paul's question addressed to them, "Did you receive the Holy

Spirit when you believed'' (19:2), is to be understood in the light of the Spirit's extraordinary charisms, as the sequel in v. 6 shows.

Their "ignorance of basic Christian matters" seems to parallel in some degree the case of Apollos "who had been instructed in the way of the Lord'' and taught accurately "the things concerning Jesus, though he knew only the baptism of John'' (18:25). Was it because Apollos "knew only the baptism of John'' that Priscilla and Aquila found it expedient to take him aside and "to explain the way of God more accurately'' (18:26)—specifically baptism(s)? The context implies as much. It is plausible, therefore, to suggest that the area in which he lacked knowledge was the same area that Paul put his finger on in the experience of the Ephesian disciples, namely, water baptism "in the name of the Lord Jesus'' and Spirit-baptism with its special charisms. In this regard, attention should be called to the stress on Apollos's forensic skills, for he was "an eloquent man . . . mighty in the Scriptures'' (18:24). His successes in Ephesus are attributed to his learning and rhetorical skill, not to the special charisms of the Spirit. In marked contrast with this is Paul's preaching "in the power of signs and wonders, in the power of the Holy Spirit'' (Rom. 15:19).

The question of John's baptism in the context is a much mooted point. Was Apollos rebaptized "in the name of the Lord Jesus,'' as were the twelve disciples later? No explicit evidence supports an argument either pro or con, although commentators have argued it both ways. Certain inferences may, however, be drawn from the context. It is explicitly stated that Apollos "knew *only* the baptism of John.'' The description parallels closely the experience of the twelve Ephesian disciples whom Paul met. Their experience was also limited to John's baptism. The fact that they were rebaptized provides an argument from analogy for Apollos's rebaptism also.

A radically different understanding of Apollos's experience is proposed by Dunn. He concludes that "unlike the twelve μαθηταί he was not re-baptized, for he differed from them in one, *the* one crucial respect: he already possessed the Spirit (18:25), whereas they did not.''[12] Here Dunn has argued for too much, for if this were true, then the "unity'' of the conversion-initiation thesis is broken. It fails to explain how John's baptism qualifies one to receive the baptism in the Spirit. He argues for his conclusion, however, by categorically affirming that "ζέων τῷ πνεύματι stands between two phrases which describe Apollos as a disciple of Jesus. It is presumably therefore itself a description of Apollos as a Christian, and πνεῦμα must be taken as (Holy) Spirit rather than (human) spirit."[13]

That apodictic "πνεῦμα must be taken as (Holy) Spirit rather than (human) spirit," does not represent an exegetical consensus. On the one hand, Gerhard Kittel supports it thus, "In the N.T. this [ζέων] is only used figuratively of being stirred by the Holy Spirit."[14] On the other hand, Bauer, Arndt, and Gingrich interpret Acts 18:25 *"with burning zeal,"* and the parallel phrase in Rom. 12:11 as *"maintain the spiritual glow."* This parallels closely the translation of both passages as *"fervent in spirit,* said of what is good."[15] In the latter instances, spirit is lower case, and thereby refers to the human spirit rather than to the Holy Spirit. F. F. Bruce is representative of the ambiguity engendered by the passage, for he renders it, "Lit(erally), 'boiling over in his spirit,' i.e., full of enthusiasm." At the same time, he acknowledges the view of Lake and Cadbury who interpret it as "boiling over with the Holy Spirit."[16]

What should not be overlooked in the context is that although Apollos "had been instructed in the way of the Lord . . . he knew [ἐπιστάμενος, was *acquainted with*][17] only the baptism of John." The context suggests that Apollos's comprehension of "the way of the Lord" was limited to the knowledge implied in John's ministry, epitomized as John's baptism. What remains unexplained in Dunn's view is how Apollos already possessed the Spirit though knowing only John's baptism. The Ephesian disciples who knew only John's baptism confessed that they had "never even heard that there is a Holy Spirit." We can only conclude that the conversion-initiation paradigm has not resolved the paradox.

In the light of the evidence, therefore, it cannot be said that "πνεῦμα *must* be taken as (Holy) Spirit." The most that can be said is that it *may* be interpreted as Holy Spirit, rather than human spirit. However, in the light of our own assessment of the context, it is our opinion that the understanding human spirit is to be preferred.

* * * * * * *

We turn our attention now to the second major strand identified by Dunn in a Pentecostal hermeneutic, "Paul's question in 19.2 seems to imply that for Paul one could be a Christian and yet not have (received) the Spirit." Taken at face value, the statement is a misrepresentation of the Pentecostal position. In a Pentecostal understanding of Luke's theology of the Spirit in Acts, one receives the Spirit for power-in-mission subsequent to the new birth. In Acts it is not the baptism in the Spirit that makes one a Christian. Rather, the Spirit is given for power-in-mission with signs following. The principal rebuttal to this position is an appeal to grammar.

The argument that the *aorist* participle πιστεύσαντες indicates an action prior to the λαμβάνειν (Riggs 53f.; Stiles 8; Miller 49; cf. Ervin 102 n 47) betrays an inadequate grasp of Greek grammar. "The action denoted by the Aorist Participle may be-
. . . antecedent to, coincident with, or subsequent to the action of the principle verb"
(E. de W. Burton, *New Testament Moods and Tenses* [1898] 59f.). Examples of the aorist participle expressing action identical with that of the main verb are Matt. 19.27 (and the numerous instances of the phrase ἀποκρίθεις εἶπεν). In Acts see 1.8; 10.33; 27.3. As most commentators recognize, πιστεύσαντες in 19.2 is a coincident aorist; it is Paul's doctrine that a man receives the Spirit when he believes.[18]

At first glance, the argument looks like a formidable, if not insurmountable, obstacle to the Pentecostal position—particularly when the Pentecostal exegetes are dismissed with a patronizing, "betrays an inadequate grasp of Greek grammar." The Pentecostal is thus made grist for the upper and the nether millstones of Greek grammar and scholarly consensus—"as most scholars recognize." This caveat invites a closer scrutiny, and this it will receive. But first, an incidental point in the exegesis above also invites a response.

The appeal to "the numerous instances of the phrase ἀποκρίθεις εἶπεν as an illustration of the coincident aorist is not to be explained by Greek syntax. It is a stylized translation of the Hebrew idiom *wayya'an lē'mor*, 'and he answered, saying.'"[19] In Hebrew the idiom is used to introduce direct discourse, and in an idiomatic translation it is left untranslated. If it were to be rendered accurately, it would be represented simply by quotation marks. The phrase itself passed into the NT from the Septuagint. It apparently resulted initially from an extremely literal translation of the Hebrew idiom by the LXX translators.

Addressing now the assertion that "The action of the Aorist Participle may be . . . antecedent to, coincident with, or subsequent to the action of the principal verb," it should be noted that A. T. Robertson emphatically denied that subsequent action is expressed by the aorist participle.[20] The exegetical choice lies between antecedent or coincident action. The choice itself raises an obvious question. If the aorist participle may be either of these—action antecedent to or coincident with the action of the main verb—what are the criteria for determining

which it is in each specific instance? Is the decision made on grammatical (the quotation above implies as much), syntactical, contextual, or
theological grounds?

Having examined a representative number of commentators on Acts
19:2, one is left with the strong impression that *theological* concerns are
the overriding ones. Hermeneutics not only informs exegesis, it dictates
the interpretation. This intuition is confirmed, in a substantive way, by
an opinion of J. H. Moulton to which F. F. Bruce calls attention thus,
"The clause 'when you believed' renders the Gk. aorist participle
πιστεύσαντες, the 'coincident aorist participle' which is *doctrinally
important. . . .*"[21]

This is a candid admission of the overriding theological considerations dictating the exegesis of Dunn, et al. Whether then Acts 19:2 is
translated "when he believes,"[22] or "after ye became believers,"[23] the
decision is "doctrinally important." In other words, the theology of the
translator and exegete is the decisive factor in the translator's choice.
Thus, the Pentecostal exegetes are exonerated of the pejorative "betrays
an inadequate grasp of Greek grammar." That is to say, the aorist
participle may be interpreted as action antecedent to or coincident with
the action of the main verb. In the final analysis, it is the theology of the
interpreter, not the grammar, that is decisive for the interpretation of the
passage.

However, the matter need not rest there and from the Pentecostal
perspective should not rest there, simply because the context has an
additional word to say. In the sequel to Paul's question, the believing
(πιστεύσαντες) is antecedent to the receiving (λαμβάνειν). The disciples *believed* before they *received* the Spirit. This is implicit in their
baptism, for the baptism of the Ephesian disciples predicated a confession of their faith in Jesus (Acts 22:16). After their baptism, "when
Paul laid his hands upon them, the Holy Spirit came on them"—their
believing is antecedent to their receiving—and the Holy Spirit announced His *coming upon* them with the special charisms characteristic
of the baptism in the Spirit in Acts, namely, "they spoke with tongues
and prophesied" (Acts 19:6). It is the contention of the Pentecostal
theologian that the *intent* of Paul's question (19:2) must be understood
in the light of the sequel, "did you receive the Holy Spirit" with signs
(tongues and prophesying) following, "after you believed?"

The third and final *strand* in a Pentecostal theology—"The time
interval between the Ephesians' baptism and Paul's laying on of hands
means that there was a time interval between conversion (which pre-

cedes baptism) and the coming of the Spirit (which followed the laying on of hands)''[24]—is really the crux of the Pentecostal position here. The rebuttal of the conversion-initiation argument begins thus, ''The argument that vv. 5f. relate to two separate procedures fails to recognize the fact that baptism and the laying on of hands here are *one* ceremony.''[25] The Pentecostal may well reply that what is touted here as a fact of the text is in fact an interpretation of the text. He would further insist that lumping together water baptism and the laying on of hands into one *ceremony* blurs the distinctive significance of each. Anyone who has received the Holy Spirit through the laying on of hands and experienced His special charisms can testify that it is far more than a ceremony. Water baptism and Spirit-baptism are distinct realities. These two baptisms are never confused in Acts.

The Holy Spirit is *present* in the conviction of sin (John 16:8; Acts 11:18), leading to repentance (Acts 11:18), and faith in Jesus Christ (Acts 14:27). This is conversion, and it culminates in water baptism. Here we would agree with Dunn that ''the most important element [in initiation] is baptism,''[26] although for different reasons. Baptism, with its concomitant public confession of faith in Jesus—''be baptized, and wash away your sins, *calling on his name*''[27] (Acts 22:16)—is a witness to the *presence* of the Holy Spirit, for ''no one can say 'Jesus is Lord' except by the Holy Spirit'' (I Cor. 12:3). The efficacy of repentance and faith in Jesus is wholly dependent on the Holy Spirit's active presence in the salvific event. Water baptism is the culmination of conversion and initiation. It does not wait upon ''the coming upon'' of the Holy Spirit with His extraordinary charisms empowering for service.

Water baptism is not, therefore, the Pentecostal *baptism in* (Acts 1:5; 11:16), *falling upon* (Acts 10:44), *coming upon* (Acts 19:6) of the Holy Spirit empowering for worldwide, agelong witness ''in the power of signs and wonders, in the power of the Spirit'' (Rom. 15:19).

What then of the laying on of hands? Is it, as Dunn proposes, only parenthetical?

The laying on of hands in v. 6 must therefore be the climax of a single ceremony whose most important element is baptism, and whose object is the reception of the Spirit. This is borne out by the form of vv. 5 f., which could be translated: '' . . . they were baptized in the name of the Lord Jesus and Paul having laid hands on them, the Holy Spirit came on them.'' The laying on of hands is almost parenthetical; the sequence of events is ''baptism (resulting in) . . . Spirit.'' Certainly the one action leads into and reaches its conclusion in the other with no discernible break.[28]

If we understand what is being said here, then the laying on of hands is incidental to the conversion-initiation process. It is an open question, however, whether or not Paul would agree that in his own experience the laying on of Ananias's hands was "almost parenthetical." But according to the above, it is fair to say that the laying on of hands is incidental to the conversion-initiation paradigm. The important thing is "baptism (resulting in) . . . Spirit." But this exposes a contradiction in the author's anti-sacramental polemic. The reception of the Spirit by the Ephesian disciples is qualitatively the same as that of Cornelius and his household. Dunn referred to the latter as "the saving, life-giving baptism in the Spirit."[29] By parity of reasoning then, the coming of the Spirit upon the Ephesian disciples is also "the saving, life-giving baptism in the Spirit." If then baptism in their case *results* in (life-giving) Spirit, does not the logic of the argument impel one to conclude that baptism does possess a sacramental efficacy?

What now of the translation of v. 5 suggested above, "they were baptized in the name of the Lord Jesus and, Paul having laid hands on them, the Holy Spirit came on them?" The critical grammatical element here is a genitive absolute, καὶ ἐπιθέντος αὐτοῖς τοῦ Παύλου χεῖρας, "And when Paul had laid his hands upon them." The genitive absolute is composed of a noun (τοῦ Παύλου), and a circumstantial participle (ἐπιθέντος) both of which are in the genitive case. Syntactically, the sentence to which this genitive absolute belongs is paratactic because it is introduced by the coordinating conjunction καὶ.

The genitive absolute may be translated several ways, for "the genitive absolute may express *time, cause*, and the like."[30] However, the temporal significance of the circumstantial participle—"And *when* Paul laid hands upon them"—is the accepted reading in most of the English versions, beginning with the Great Bible (1540) through the New International Version (1973). This temporal significance underscores the *sequential* rather than the parenthetical nature of the actions related in the text. The laying on of Paul's hands is not an episode merely parenthetical to "baptism (resulting in) . . . Spirit." It is a link between conversion-initiation and the receiving of the Holy Spirit for power-in-mission. The sequence is baptism = conversion-initiation followed by the laying on of hands for the reception of the Spirit = power-in-mission.

The following conclusions summarize our response to Dunn's arguments.

1. The contrast between οἱ μαθηταί and τινες μαθηταί is irrelevant to the identity of the Ephesian disciples in Acts 19:1ff. The contrast is

both arbitrary and contrived, and is without support from the context. It does not establish the conclusion that "the twelve did not belong to 'the disciples' in Ephesus."

2. The argument for a coincident aorist participle, πιστεύσαντες (Acts 19:2), is grammatically inconclusive. It does not establish the thesis that saving-faith and the baptism in the Spirit are coterminous in Acts. In the final analysis, it is the interpreter's theology that plays a decisive role in interpreting the participle in the text.

3. The attempt to make the laying on of hands merely parenthetical to the conversion-initiation process falls into the category of special pleading. Conversion-initiation culminates in water baptism. The laying on of hands subsequent to water baptism is for the reception of the Holy Spirit for power-in-mission.

Notes

[1]Dunn, op. cit., pp. 83–89.

[2]Ibid., p. 83.

[3]Ibid., p. 85.

[4]Ibid., p. 84.

[5]Ibid.

[6]Ibid.

[7]Ibid.

[8]Ibid.

[9]Ibid.

[10]This and the following quotes are from the NASB.

[11]Dunn, op. cit., p. 84.

[12]Ibid., p. 88.

[13]Ibid.

[14]Theological Dictionary of the New Testament II, trans. by Geoffrey W. Bromiley (Grand Rapids: Wm. B. Eerdmans, 1964), p. 875.

[15]Joseph Henry Thayer, trans., A Greek-English Lexicon of the New Testament (New York: American Book Company, [1886]).

[16]The Acts of the Apostles (Grand Rapids: Wm. B. Eerdmans, 1960), p. 351.

[17]Bauer, Arndt, and Gingrich.

[18]Dunn, op. cit., pp. 86, 87.

[19]Cf. LXX Gen. 23:10; 41:16; Josh. 1:16; cf. also the cognate εἶπεν λέγων.

[20]A Grammar of the Greek New Testament in the Light of Historical Research (Nashville: Broadman Press, 1934), p. 861.

[21]Commentary on the Book of the Acts, The New International Commentary on the New Testament (Grand Rapids: Wm. B. Eerdmans, 1964), p. 385, n. 8; italics added.

[22]Dunn, et al.

[23]Heinrich August Wilhelm Meyer, Critical and Exegetical Handbook to the Acts of the Apostles, trans. William P. Dickson (New York: Funk & Wagnalls, 1883), p. 365.

[24]Dunn, op. cit., p. 83.

[25]Ibid., p. 87.

[26]Ibid.

[27]Italics added.

[28]Dunn, op. cit., p. 87.

[29]Ibid., p. 81.

[30]Henry Lamar Crosby and John Nevin Schaeffer, *An Introduction to Greek* (New York: Allyn and Bacon [1928]) p. 72.

Chapter 8

Conversion-Initiation in Acts

"Conversion-Initiation in the Acts of the Apostles"[1] is a synthesis and restatement of previous assumptions and conclusions. Since these have already been examined in some detail, any attempt to respond to each particular would be needlessly repetitious. There are, however, three statements of the hypothesis that invite response because of the grammatical and theological problems involved.

1. There have been recurrent references to Acts 2:38 as a normative pattern for conversion-initiation, "the only verse in Acts which directly relates to one another the three most important elements in conversion-initiation: Repentance, water-baptism, and the gift of the Spirit."[2] The most important of these elements is the gift of the Spirit, for

The Spirit is the bearer of salvation, for the promise of 2.38 must include the promise of 2.21 (and 16.31) . . . the deliverance "in those days" Peter interprets of eschatological salvation in 2.21 and the gift of the Spirit in 2.38.[3]

The conclusion as stated rests upon a selective use of the context, for if "the promise of 2:38 must include the promise of 2:21," then it may be argued just as cogently that it must also include "the promise" in 1:4, i.e., the baptism in the Spirit for power-in-mission (cf. 1:5, 8). It must also include "the promise" in 2:33, namely, "this which you see and hear," notably "tongues" (2:4). Consistency requires that "the promise" of 2:38 must be interpreted in the light of all the references to "the promise" in the context.

Furthermore, the suggested parallelism, "eschatological salvation" (2:21) = "the gift of the Spirit" (2:38), is misleading. If the "Repent, and be baptized" (2:38) parallels "eschatological salvation" (2:21), then the "gift of the Holy Spirit" (2:38) must parallel the pouring out of the Spirit (2:17)—but upon whom?

Luke's quotation of Joel 2:28ff. is a free rendering of the Septuagint text. The clause, "this is what was spoken by the prophet Joel" (Acts 2:16), is intended to identify the events of Pentecost with Joel's prophecy, and the phenomena accompanying the Spirit's coming at Pentecost are anticipated in the charisms promised in the prophecy of Joel. In Acts 2:17, the Spirit is poured out on "your sons and your daughters" accompanied by the charisms of prophesying, visions, and dreams. In Acts 2:18 the outpouring of the Spirit is "on my menservants and my maidservants," with the charism of prophesying promised as its accompaniment.

Contextually there is every reason to understand the phrases, "your sons and your daughters," and "my menservants and my maidservants" as synonymous expressions referring to the same group of people, namely, the children of Israel. The outpouring of the Spirit (2:17ff.) would not make them what they already were, "sons and daughters" (2:17), "menservants and maidservants" (2:18). Rather it would empower them with the charisms of the Holy Spirit. In Peter's application of Joel's prophecy to the disciples, the Pentecostal baptism in the Spirit did not make them what they already were, "sons and daughters," "menservants and maidservants." It empowered them with the charisms of the Spirit. Consistent with this context, those who call upon the name of the Lord (2:21), who repent and are baptized (2:38), become thereby "sons and daughters," "menservants and maidservants." The "gift of the Holy Spirit" is given (subsequently) to empower them with the charisms of the Spirit. As Johannes Munck has succinctly said, "the pouring of the Spirit over them all stresses that this happened to the whole Christian congregation in Jerusalem."[4] The conversion-initiation schema has consistently ignored the clear charismatic dimension of Spirit-baptism that distinguishes "the gift of the Holy Spirit" from conversion-initiation.

We conclude, therefore, that the Spirit's coming upon sons and daughters, menservants and maidservants, cannot be conversion-initiation. Dunn's parallelism fails of consistency in the light of the context.

It is appropriate here to point out that the theory of conversion-initiation represents a theological reductionism designed to harmonize the Johannine theology of regeneration with the Lukan theology of power. It is significant to note that in John's theology of the Spirit, he does not use the distinctively Lukan word δύναμις, "power." It is equally significant that in Luke's theology of the Spirit (with the exception of the nativity narrative), the characteristic Johannine word γεννάω, "to beget," is not used. In John's Gospel receiving Jesus by faith results in spiritual rebirth (ἐκ θεοῦ ἐγεννήθησαν, "begotten of God," John 1:13). The new birth is the Spirit's gift given at conversion. On the other hand, for Luke "the gift of the Holy Spirit" is given to the people of God, who receive power thereby (λήμψεσθε δύναμιν, Acts

1:8) to witness *"in the power* of signs and wonders, in the power of the Spirit" (Rom. 15:19).[5] To attribute regeneration to "the gift of the Holy Spirit" in Acts 2:38, 39 is as alien to Luke's doctrine of the Spirit (2:21 is a quotation from Joel accommodated to Luke's purpose) as it is to impute power to John's. It is exegetically indefensible to put Johannine categories in Luke's mouth, and vice versa.

In the Pentecostal pneumatology, John's theology of the Spirit as a new spiritual life is the presupposition for Luke's theology of the Spirit as spiritual power. Consistency requires then that Peter's words, "repent . . . be baptized . . . and you shall receive the gift of the Holy Spirit," be interpreted in the categories of Luke's theology of power, rather than in that of John's doctrine of regeneration. From the Pentecostal point of view, it is a serious category mistake to read conversion-initiation, with its concomitant Johannine doctrine of the new birth, into Luke's "gift of the Holy Spirit" for power-in-mission.

Conversion and initiation as understood by Pentecostals and other Evangelicals is "repentance toward God and faith in our Lord Jesus Christ" (Acts 20:21), followed by water baptism. Understood in terms of the Johannine theology of regeneration, the birth from above (ἄνωθεν, John 3:3) is the divine grace received through faith. Luke's *gift* of the Holy Spirit is to empower Christians for life and service. In the conversion-initiation hypothesis, John's doctrine of the new birth and Luke's doctrine of empowerment are treated as one and the same. To the Pentecostal this is an artificial harmonization that does not do justice either to John or to Luke. In the Pentecostal view both John and Luke speak of distinct operations of the Holy Spirit that are not to be conflated arbitrarily. The Lukan gift of the Spirit is logically subsequent to conversion and initiation in the order of salvation. Its distinguishing characteristics are the supernatural charisms of the Spirit that reveal His power in operation.

It is here (Acts 2:38, 39), at the point of Peter's reply to the inquiry of the multitudes at Pentecost, that Dunn's disagreement with Pentecostals comes into sharpest focus. For the former, repentance, faith, water baptism, and the gift of the Spirit are subsumed into one conversion-initiation process that represents an unbreakable unity. In the present context of the discussion, this raises another question. It is clear from Luke's account in Acts that reception of the Spirit was accompanied by the audible phenomena of tongues and prophesying. These provided objective criteria by which the *gift* of the Spirit was distinguished. In the conversion-initiation paradigm, we are not told how one may *know* that they have received the *gift* of the Holy Spirit. One must assume, in the absence of a statement to the contrary, that this implies an inner intuition without objective verification.

It is precisely at this point that the Pentecostal must fault the conversion-initiation schema as scripturally and theologically inadequate. In Acts the reception of the *gift* of the Spirit is not simply a subjective, intuitive awareness of the Spirit's presence, for tongues and prophesying (Acts 2:4; 10:45, 46; 19:6) are objective (and the Pentecostal would add, normative) witnesses to the reception of the *gift* of the Spirit. They are *not*, however, evidence of the new birth. It is our personal opinion that the fruit(s) of the Spirit (Gal. 5:22) are the evidence of the new birth, for in the order of nature fruit is a consequence of life. In the spiritual order (super-nature), they are the attributes of the divine nature of which believers become partakers in regeneration. (II Peter 1:4).

If then the vocal charisms of tongues and prophesying are the objective witness to the reception of the *gift* of the Holy Spirit, when and why did this pattern change—if indeed it has changed? The Pentecostal would affirm both biblically and experientially that is has not changed—the dispensational argument notwithstanding.

2. The second assertion of the conversion-initiation argument, to which we have chosen to respond, discusses "the relation between faith, the act of believing into (πιστεύσαι εἰς) Christ, and the gift of the Spirit."[6] In his development of this thesis, it is not only Pentecostals, but also what is described as "the classic Reformed position"[7] that is challenged.

Much of our argument so far may have failed to convince Pentecostals, most of whom seem to hold what to them is the classic Reformed view of the order of salvation, namely, that the Spirit works in or with a person prior to his conversion, enabling him to repent and believe, at which point he receives Jesus into his heart and life. To these two distinct works of grace the Pentecostal adds a third in his theology of the baptism in the Spirit.[8]

A subsequent comment is even more specific, if that is possible, for it is said that "Many conservative theologians take the classic Reformed position to be that in the *ordo salutis* regeneration precedes conversion and is that which enables a man to convert."[9]

Excursus on the Image of God

Inasmuch as I find myself in substantive disagreement with both of these views, a personal digression is in order. I cannot answer for what others may, or may not, believe about conversion. I do, however, reject the view that "regeneration precedes conversion and is that which enables a man to convert." There is a middle ground to both the "Reformed" view and Dunn's view. It takes as its point of departure the doctrine of the image of God in which man was created. Just what constitutes the image of God in man is not defined in Scripture, but this is not to imply that theologians may not postulate such definitions descriptively, analogically, and existentially. Such discussions are not germane to our immediate concern. A theological construct relating to the image is, however, important to the present discussion, that is, the recognition of the category of freedom in respect of man's will and the effects of the Fall upon it.

The biblical account makes it clear that the image replicates the divine likeness within the limits of man's creaturehood. The divine-human relationship is not, therefore, a symbiotic one. Rather, the similitude of the image predicates a mutuality of being in both God and man. The "Fall" of man marred and defaced the image of God in man. It did not, however, destroy it. Were the image of God eradicated in man because of his Fall, man would still be a creature made by God but no longer a creature created in the image of God. Symbiosis would then be the only possible relationship between God and man-as-mere-creature. It is, therefore, the image of God, even in "fallen" man, that provides the ground of addressability to which the saving word is spoken.

While the image is more than man's faculties, the saving word addresses man intellectually, emotionally, and volitionally, and man is responsible (even in his fallen state) for his response. The Fall did not destroy either the will of man, or his accountability before God. In the *Spiritual Homilies* attributed to St. Macarius of Egypt, the image of God is presented, in part, as "the formal condition of liberty, free will, the faculty of choice which cannot be destroyed by sin."[10] Over against the "Reformed" view, I would agree with Dunn when he says, "Man's act in conversion is to repent, to turn and to believe."[11] I would also agree with Dunn in his interpretation of what he calls "the classic Reformed view of the order of salvation, namely, that the Spirit works in or with a person prior to his conversion, enabling him to repent and believe, at which point he receives Jesus into his heart and life." Receiv(ing) Jesus into his heart and life" is concomitant with the Spirit's work in regeneration, for he who receives and believes is born of God (John 1:11–13).

The interaction of the Holy Spirit with the human will in convicting of sin (John 16:8) is not proof that regeneration precedes conversion. It is, however, prerequisite to authentic conversion, for conversion without repudiation of sin is no conversion at all. Through the revealed word (Scripture), the Spirit mediates an encounter with the incarnate, glorified Word (Jesus Christ). Conversion *from* sin *to* the Savior is an affirmative response (i.e., repentance and faith) to the divine address. The divine grace vouchsafed to repentance and faith is the new birth.

While I can agree with Dunn when he says, "Much of our argument so far may have failed to convince Pentecostals"—for his arguments have not convinced—my rationale is a decidedly different one. In fact, not only am I unconvinced, but the presentation of the conversion-initiation thesis to this point has served only to confirm my confidence in the correctness of the Pentecostal hermeneutics—and this for two reasons.

a. The first reason is well stated by Gordon Fee in his review of Dunn's *Baptism in the Holy Spirit*. "What is of interest," he writes, "is that the conclusions noted above may be found in the introduction; one wonders at times whether they do not also precede the exegesis."[12] As I have repeatedly pointed out, at crucial points his exegesis has not only failed to convince, it has been prejudiced by special pleading.

b. The attempt to disprove the Pentecostal position by focusing exclusively on its doctrine is another serious category mistake. I cannot help feeling that Dunn has not truly understood the nature of the Pentecostal phenomenon itself. This emerges rather clearly in a remark relative to a statement by Bruner which he quotes, obviously with approval, "If, then, Bruner is correct in saying 'the truth of Pentecostalism's doctrine of the Spirit rests or falls on the exegesis of the knotty pneumatic passages in Acts' (43) our conclusion can only be that the doctrine falls."[13] But what both Bruner and Dunn have failed to realize is that "Pentecostalism" cannot be disposed of simply by an attack upon its doctrine, for the Pentecostal witness is *both* an experience and a doctrine. If it is to be discredited, then the experience as well as the doctrine must be proven false. Here the instincts, if not the rhetoric, of those who invoke the *ad hominem* argument against the Pentecostal experience, as in itself false, are closer to understanding the true nature of the case. They have at least recognized that, if the Pentecostal doctrine is to be proven wrong, the Pentecostal experience must also be discredited.

* * * * * * *

The crux of the exposition of "the relation between faith, the act of believing into Christ . . . and the gift of the Spirit" is set forth in the following words:

I do not deny that the Christian theologian may quite properly speak of the convicting work of the Spirit prior to and leading up to conversion (even if John 16:11, and perhaps I Cor. 14:24., are about the only passages which can be quoted in support). However, I affirm most emphatically that for the NT writers who speak on this matter, the gift of saving grace which the individual receives in conversion, that is, on believing, is the Holy Spirit. The decisive gift of the Spirit, which makes a man a Christian and without which he is no Christian, comes neither before nor after conversion, but *in* conversion. The NT knows of no prior reception.''[14]

The categorical assertion that ''The NT knows of no prior reception'' (of the Spirit) is in marked contrast to a concession made in the discussion of the ''Johannine Pentecost.'' Therein it is conceded that, at least for the apostles, the Paschal impartation of the Spirit (John 20:22) came *before* they received the Pentecostal gift of the Spirit. This is dismissed, however, as a dispensationally exceptional case, one not to be repeated. In the appropriate place, we will argue that there is no biblical justification for this dispensational expedient. We will further argue that the apostolic experience of the Paschal impartation of the Spirit, followed by the Pentecostal baptism in the Spirit for power-in-mission, is a norm for subsequent generations of believers. This, in and of itself, constitutes a substantive challenge to the apodictic affirmation that the gift of the Spirit ''comes neither before nor after conversion but in conversion.''

3. The third restatement of the conversion-initiation hypothesis to which we offer a response is a rejection of the Pentecostal doctrine of evangelism. Pentecostals share with the majority of Evangelicals the understanding that ''receiving Christ'' is at the heart of NT evangelism. Nevertheless, Dunn claims that here, too, they are wrong.

The Pentecostal attempt to evade the NT emphasis by distinguishing the acceptance of Jesus at conversion from the later gift of the Spirit is in fact a departure from NT teaching. For the NT *nowhere* speaks of conversion as ''receiving Christ'' (despite the frequent use of this phrase in popular evangelism).[15]

The assertion that ''the NT *nowhere* speaks of conversion as 'receiving Christ''' is a sweeping one. It places Dunn at odds with all Evangelicals, as well as Pentecostals. Having scored Pentecostals, Catholics, and now Evangelicals, one wonders who really meets the criteria of the conversion-initiation hypothesis? However, before this claim can be entertained seriously, certain direct references in John and Paul to the contrary must be explained (or explained away). This task is undertaken in the following words:

John 1.12 refers primarily to the historical welcome which a few of ''his own'' gave him, in contrast to the rejection of the many (1.11f.; cf. 5.43; 6.21; 13.20). In Col. 2.6 the word used is παραλαμβάνω which properly means the receiving of a heritage or tradition; Paul reminds the Colossians how they received the proclamation of Jesus as Lord (Arndt and Gingrich)—since Jesus was delivered to you as Christ and Lord (NEB).[16]

The verb παραλαμβάνω is used in John 1:11, while its cognate, λαμβάνω is used *in the same sense* in 1.12 (cf. John 13:20). In John 1:11, it does *not* mean the "receiving of a heritage or tradition." It refers rather to the receiving of the person of Jesus. Whether it is the "receiving" of the historical Jesus, or the glorified Christ, the distinction is entirely beside the point. What the text does illustrate is the usage of παραλαμβάνω with the accusative of persons, and this we will argue is significant also for its meaning in Col. 2:6.

Before proceeding directly to a consideration of Col. 2:6, it is important to evaluate the claim that "John 1:12 refers primarily to the historical welcome which a few of 'his own' gave him, in contrast to the rejection of the many." While it obviously ignores the context, the purpose of this remark is to support the earlier contention that "the NT *nowhere* speaks of conversion as 'receiving Christ.'" A substantive distinction is thereby implied between the historical Jesus—and the relationship of His disciples to Him, and the glorified Christ—and the relationship of subsequent believers to Him. The intent of the assertion is clear. If it can be shown that John 1:12 refers merely to the receiving of the historical Jesus by His contemporaries, then the salvific encounter with Christ is eliminated from the context. But once again, the context refuses to conform to the assumptions of the conversion-initiation thesis.

Receiving Jesus in the context of John 1:11–13 is another way of saying conversion. Whether it is the historical Jesus, or the glorified Christ, is irrelevant to the argument. The result, for those "who received him, who believed in his name," was (1) "the right *to become* the children of God" and (2) the new birth, "who were *born* (again) . . . of God."[17]

What now of the assertion that παραλαμβάνω "properly speaking means the receiving of a heritage or tradition?" As we have seen above, John 1:11–13 is an exception to the rule, if a rule it be. Nor is this the exception that proves the rule, for Col. 2:6 is a second witness that confirms the fact that παραλαμβάνω is used of "receiving Christ" in conversion. Syntactically, both of these passages differ substantively from the use of the verb in Mark 7:4; I Cor. 11:23; 15:1, 3; Gal. 1:9, 12; Phil. 4:9; Col. 4:17; I Thess. 4:1; II Thess. 3:6; and Heb. 12:28. In all of these instances, the object of παραλαμβάνω is *impersonal*. In Col.

2:6, as in John 1:11–13, the object of the verb is *personal*, "As therefore you received Christ Jesus the Lord ('Ὡς οὖν παρελάβετε τὸν Χριστὸν 'Ιησοῦν)." The Colossian believers received more than a "proclamation of him as Lord," Bauer, Arndt, and Gingrich notwithstanding. They received a person, Christ Jesus himself, at their conversion. Paul's added exhortation to them to "walk in *him*"[18] (2:6), supports this observation.

Receiving Christ at conversion is consistent with Paul's doctrine of the mystical union of the believer with Christ. For instance in Gal. 2:20, for the Apostle Paul, "it is no longer I who live, but Christ who lives in me." In the Colossian epistle this theme of mystical union with Christ—"Christ in you, the hope of glory" (1:27)—anticipates its recurrence in 2:6. Paul's doctrine of the mystical union of Christ with the believer bespeaks a substantive spiritual experience beginning with conversion. It transcends the verbal symbols and metaphors in which is is couched and ultimately defies definition; nevertheless, it is to be reckoned with exegetically, if one is to do justice to Paul's thought here.

Dunn concludes his argument with a confusing bit of theologizing. He says without qualification, "What one receives at conversion is the Spirit and life of the risen exalted Christ."[19] Read in the light of the previous claim—"the NT *nowhere* speaks of conversion as 'receiving Christ'"—this latter assertion compounds the christological ambiguities already encountered in his arguments. Does this suggest that in conversion "the Spirit and life of the risen exalted Christ" somehow function independently of His person? Is it a covert Nestorianizing tendency? Is there here a dichotomy between "the Spirit and life of the risen exalted Christ" and Christ himself in the economy of redemption? Does this suggest that the Incarnation somehow limits Jesus Christ to the physical laws of time and space? That is to say, He is *there* (risen and exalted), while His spirit and life function *here*? These exegetical and theological ambiguities reinforce our conclusion that one does "receive Christ" in conversion.

Notes

1Dunn, op. cit., pp. 90–102.
2Ibid., p. 91.
3Ibid., p. 92.
4Johannes Munck *The Acts of the Apostles*, Vol. 31, *The Anchor Bible*, Rev. William F. Albright and C. S. Mann (Garden City: Doubleday & Company Inc., 1973), p.18.
5NASB, italics added.

[6]Dunn, op. cit., p. 93.

[7]Ibid., p. 94.

[8]Ibid., p. 93.

[9]Ibid., p. 94.

[10]Vladimir Lossky, *The Mystical Theology of the Eastern Church* (1957; rpt. Cambridge: James Clarke & Co., 1968), pp. 115, 116.

[11]Dunn, op. cit., p. 96.

[12]Gordon D. Fee, *Journal of Biblical Literature*, 91 (March 1972): 128, 129.

[13]Dunn, op. cit., p.96.

[14]Ibid., pp. 94, 95.

[15]Ibid., p. 95.

[16]Ibid.

[17]NASB, italics added.

[18]Ibid.

[19]Dunn, op. cit., p. 95.

Chapter 9

Paul's Early Epistles

The discussion of "The Early Paulines"[1] begins with a nuanced but, nonetheless, disparaging bit of anti-Pentecostal rhetoric.

Pentecostalism is built foursquare on Acts. So far as its doctrine of Spirit-baptism is concerned Paul need not have written anything. Indeed Paul seems to be more of an embarrassment than an asset, so that time and again expositions of this doctrine conveniently ignore him, apart from a few face-saving references which are not always relevant to the doctrine as such. Two exceptions are usually I Cor. 12.13 and Eph. 1.13, which by means of often rather superficial exegesis are taken to confirm the doctrine already extracted from Acts.[2]

These comments, while unilaterally deprecating the theological sophistication and/or exegetical competence of Pentecostal theologians, inadvertently betray the author's failure to understand the experiential, as well as the propositional, nature of the Pentecostal rationale. Of course the Pentecostal recognizes the significance of Acts for the *experiential* and *phenomenological* descriptions of the Pentecostal experience. As a matter of fact, any hermeneutic that fails to take account of the historical and phenomenological aspects of the experience will not understand either Luke or Paul.

Even a casual reading of Paul's epistles makes it clear that he does not describe the historical event of Pentecost. But it is a methodological error to argue from his silence on this point that it is not a basic presupposition in his theology of the Spirit. His own experiences on the Damascus road, and later in Damascus, would negate such an assumption. His interest, however, seems to lie in theologizing the significance of the Spirit's presence in the ongoing experience of the Christian. He does not, therefore, distinguish explicitly between the Spirit's action in conversion and baptism in the Spirit for power-in-mission, although both motifs may be discerned in his writings.

Spirit-baptism is a distinctively Lukan metaphor. Only in I Cor. 12:13 is there evidence, though debatable, for a Pauline use of this figure of speech. However, even when it is granted that Paul here uses Lukes's metaphor, it cannot be concluded that Paul uses it in the same sense as does Luke. Where similarity of phrasing by different authors does occur, it is the responsibility of the interpreter to discern whether the relationship is substantive or merely verbal. This touches a sensitive nerve in the conversion-initiation argument, for, as we shall point out, significant semantic ambiguities cloud the case for this hypothesis in the present discussion.

A semantic ambiguity is seen in Dunn's frequent use of the phrase "the gift of the Spirit"—nine times in his chapter where he discusses this issue—as synonymous with conversion-initiation. Once again it must be recalled that this is not a generically Pauline idiom, but it is characteristic of Luke's terminology in Acts, where it is synonymous with the baptism in/filling with/gift of the Holy Spirit for power-in-mission.

These ambiguities raise an interesting methodological problem for the conversion-initiation hypothesis. It has already been argued, albeit not convincingly, that the gift of the Holy Spirit in Acts 2:38 is a *crux interpretum* for the theory. As we have already noted, implicit in this argument is an arbitrary concordance between John's new-birth theology of the Spirit, and Luke's theology of power-in-mission. This is not precisely the point at issue here. However, what is at issue, from a methodological standpoint, is this: Does not this repeated use of the Lukan metaphor, the gift of the Spirit, in a Pauline context impose a semantic harmonization of the two that, from a Pentecostal point of view, is not supported by contextual exegesis? The question is more than rhetorical. Does not this methodology covertly impose an arbitrary normalization upon these two contexts without regard for their distinctive emphases? From a pragmatic standpoint, if not from an exegetical one, it has a certain polemic value, for the derogation of the Pentecostal exegesis of Luke/Acts sets the stage to make Paul's theology of the Spirit (?) normative for the interpretation of Luke/Acts, to the disparagement of both Pentecostal and sacramentalist.

Inasmuch as the Pentecostals have, in Dunn's opinion, either ignored or misused Paul, the burden of his effort in this chapter is directed against sacramentalists. In this he is quite explicit.

This means that, while our primary task will be to examine the role of the Spirit and the gift of the Spirit in conversion-initiation, most of the actual debate will not be with Pentecostals but with sacramentalists, who, generally speaking, have found in Paul a richer, more satisfying picture than the one presented by Luke."[3]

By asking, "How are we going to set about discovering Paul's mind on the subject?" i.e., of baptism, he raises an important methodological question. He answers by saying:

It would be easy to decide on a hypothesis, and then to begin with those passages which best support that hypothesis. The other, more 'difficult' and more 'obscure' passages ('difficult' and 'obscure' so far as the hypothesis is concerned, of course) can then be interpreted in the light of the clear passages.[4]

In scoring as defective many modern treatments of baptism for their "failure to appreciate the fact that baptism is only one element in the total complex event of becoming a Christian,"[5] he has himself formulated a conversion-initiation hypothesis that predetermines his exegesis. Focusing attention on texts that bear immediately on baptism, in his opinion, "*necessarily* distorts the total picture."[6] He finds it also highly questionable "the way in which the gift of the Spirit is time and again subordinated to and interpreted in the light of baptism."[7] But is it not equally questionable to subordinate the gift of the Spirit and baptism to a preconceived conversion-initiation hypothesis?

Within a Pentecostal frame of reference, the charge of subordination of the *gift* of the Spirit to baptism is another semantic ambiguity. If the distinction between the Johannine doctrine of the regenerative action of the Spirit and the Lukan doctrine of the gift of the Spirit for power-in-mission is observed, then the claim of subordination of the (Lukan) *gift* of the Spirit to baptism is simply another category mistake.

The conclusion Dunn derives from the foregoing is that "it is needlessly misleading to speak of 'baptismal contexts' [or of Spirit—or faith—contexts for that matter]."[8] His rationale for this conclusion is that Paul speaks of baptism without mentioning the Spirit or faith, and faith without including a reference to the Spirit or baptism, or again the gift of the Spirit without alluding to faith and baptism.[9]

The tenor of these remarks raises the specter of a procrustean exegesis in conformity with the conversion-initiation hypothesis. This intuition is confirmed by this additional remark, "What we want are conversion-initiation contexts, *whatever elements are present or absent*."[10] Obviously the missing elements are to be supplied by the application of the conversion-initiation paradigm. This implies considerable dependence on an analogical method, reinforced, as we shall see, by frequent appeals to the argument from silence.

Excursus on a World-View

The burden of Dunn's chapter, as noted above, is directed against sacramentalists. The intuition that Pentecostals and sacramentalists share a common ground is a sound one but for reasons which may not be apparent in a propositional exposition. In our own experience, we have often observed that many previously nonsacramental Pentecostals/ Charismatics have been, in varying degrees, attracted to a sacramental theology as a result of their Pentecostal experience. When understood existentially, this change in orientation is quite understandable. An experiential encounter with the charismata of the Holy Spirit presents a disturbing challenge to prior theological categories predicated upon an implicit dichotomy between Spirit and matter. The result is frequently a theological reorientation away from a rationalistic (Platonic!) symbolism and toward a sacramental realism. It is this existential dimension of Pentecostal sacramentalism that makes it difficult to find a common ground with a propositionally conceived antisacramental metaphysics.

Sacramentalism and antisacramentalism are essentially two antithetical statements about the nature of reality. Each operates within its own philosophical/theological assumptions about the fundamental nature of that reality. Failure to enunciate clearly that the conversion-initiation paradigm is, in itself, an a priori hypothesis carries over into the polemic against sacramentalists. Here too, unacknowledged assumptions dictate the exegesis.

For the sacramentalist the created order is an open one. It is a Spirit/ matter continuum, after the analogy of a matter/energy continuum, in which water, wine, and bread become vehicles of the Spirit's presence and activity. For the antisacramentalist, man exists in an essentially closed order of creation. Spirit and matter are logically quantified into discontinuous, even antithetical, spheres of God's presence and activity. However, even for the antisacramentalist, these spheres of God's presence and activity intersect historically in the Incarnation. In the Incarnation, Spirit assumed material form, and thereby matter itself became a modality of divine presence and redemptive activity in the created order. For the Christian, all sacramental reality flows from this fundamental premise.

In the Incarnation, the divine Word assumed human flesh and thereby mediated the presence and saving action of God to man. In the proclamation of the Word, the Word-that-became-flesh becomes (propositional) Word, and the debate between sacramentalist and antisacramentalist intersects at this point. For the latter, God's presence is now subsumed in the flesh-become-(propositional) Word. As propositional Word, the presence of God is objectified in the words of human speech. In a nonsacramental schema of grace, therefore, the flesh-become-Word-again addresses the numinous dimension of man's existence in rationally conceived categories of presence and activity. Thus the presence and activity of the flesh-become-Word-again is limited to symbolic address, and the role of the Spirit in such a paradigm is circumscribed by the propositional nature of the address. As a consequence, the sacramental presence of the Word-that-became-flesh is circumscribed by the *symbolic* address of the flesh-become-Word-again.

The dichotomy in the antisacramentalist's paradigm of reality reduces divine presence and activity in the natural order to a subjective immanence. The objective presence and activity of God in His supernatural charisms is either explained away as a dispensational once-and-for-all, or projected into the suprahistorical consciousness of the community, or denied altogether.

It is at this point that the Pentecostal shares common ground with the sacramentalist, for the phenomenology of the Pentecostal experience precludes quantifying reality into discontinuous spheres of Spirit and matter. Thus a consistent application of the Pentecostal pneumatology places the Pentecostal on the side of the sacramentalist, for in a paradigm of a Spirit/matter continuum, water, wine, and bread may indeed become sacramental modalities of the divine presence.

* * * * * * *

In the critique of the following passages, the reader will be reminded repeatedly that the conversion-initiation paradigm predetermines the exegesis.

I Thess. 1:5–9; 2:13

Three elements in the conversion-initiation schema are identified, "The elements in conversion-initiation of which Paul speaks here are: The Word preached, the response of faith, and the Holy Spirit."[11] Repentance and baptism are not mentioned. The manner in which the Spirit is received is not related, and even the time of reception is problematical, "Paul does not say how or when they received the Spirit, although the reception of the Spirit *seems* to be closely linked to the reception of the Word."[12] The references in the text are so generalized that no order of conversion-initiation can be deduced from them. The conclusion is hypothetical, and buttressed by the argument from silence.

I Thess. 4:7–8

In this passage only two of the elements in the conversion-initiation thesis are pinpointed, "God's call is effectual because it comes in the Word of God which the Spirit applies powerfully to the conscience and heart of man so that he responds to the call by receiving the Word and the Spirit."[13] The immediate subject under discussion in this text is sanctification. Repentance, faith, and baptism are not mentioned. Once again the references are too generalized to reconstruct a conversion-initiation paradigm from them.

II Thess. 2:13–14

The subject of this text is the divine purpose in election. Two of the conversion-initiation components are stressed, "we see highlighted the two chief means to and elements in being saved: The operation of the Spirit in setting apart, and the operation of the individual in believing the truth proclaimed in the Gospel."[14] It is pointedly observed here that "Water-baptism is entirely absent from Thessalonians"[15]—but repentance is also absent from Thessalonians. One cannot help wondering (aloud) whether the conversion-initiation theory is an exegesis of the Word of God, or an eisegesis of the silence of God.

Gal. 2:16–21

It is stated here categorically that "There is no doubt that we have here a conversion-initiation passage (2:16), but it is not an exposition of water-baptism."[16] It is conceded, however, that "If water-baptism is not mentioned neither is the Spirit. Yet the work of the Spirit is *implied* more strongly than the rite of baptism."[17] It should be added that repentance is also omitted. Apparently a need is felt to explain the absence of the Spirit from what is claimed for a conversion-initiation passage. The reason offered is purely conjectural, "The Spirit *probably* does not feature here because Paul wishes to put his primary emphasis on Christ."[18]

Having identified the sacramentalist as his adversary in this chapter, Dunn's first explicit rebuttal of Pentecostals comes in a summary remark, a continuation of the preceding quotation. Addressing Pentecostals he says, "but so far as the Pentecostal is concerned, it must be emphasized that the moment when Christ began to 'live in me' cannot be distinguished from the reception of the Spirit who is the life of 'Christ in me.'"[19]

So far as the Pentecostal is concerned, the tautology here tells nothing of Paul's experience. He would simply reply that Paul's *words* must be interpreted in the light of his pneumatic *experience*. For this we must rely on Luke's description in Acts 9. There Paul's reception of the Holy Spirit, through the laying on of Ananias's hands, is not described as a new birth, but as a filling with the Spirit, a metaphor that in the context of Acts is synonymous with the baptism in the Spirit for power-in-mission.

Gal. 3:1–5, 14

Dunn's "crushing rejoinder to Pentecostal ideas about the reception of the Spirit"[20] is meaningful rhetoric only if one accepts his conversion-initiation hypothesis. Paul knows of only one reception of the Spirit. From the Pentecostal standpoint, it is a recapitulation of assumptions and arguments to which we have responded above.

Conspicuously absent in the exposition of the passage is an exegesis of 3:5, "he who supplies, ὁ ἐπιχορηγῶν (*continuously*), the Spirit to you and *works miracles* among you." As already noted, the charismatic phenomenology of Spirit-baptism has been consistently avoided in the exposition of the conversion-initiation thesis. The passage clearly documents Paul's awareness of the reception of the Spirit for power-in-mission.

The conversion-initiation elements here are "preaching, faith, and the Spirit,"[21] of which "Faith alone is the critical factor on the human side."[22] From the sacramental standpoint, the reader is once again informed that "The most significant thing about water-baptism here is that it is not mentioned,"[23] but then neither is repentance.

Gal. 3:26–27

Picking up again on the sacramental motif, the discussion of βαπτίζειν εἰς Χριστόν (3:26f.) leaves unanswered the sacramental question addressed here. While acknowledging that the passage refers to water-baptism, it is characterized as a metaphor "to describe the entry of the believer into Christian experience,"[24] but this leaves unanswered the connection, if any, between the metaphor and the rite. There is an unmistakable impression that metaphor translates here as symbol and represents only an analogical relationship between symbolic rite and spiritual reality. This is acknowledged in so many words, "The rite provides and lies behind the metaphor, but we cannot say from Gal. 3.26f. that it effects what it thus figuratively describes."[25] But from a grammatical standpoint, it cannot be asserted that it does *not* effect what it describes. The conclusion proceeds from the author's theological assumptions. It is not a necessary exegetical conclusion. On the other hand, in a Pentecostal hermeneutic that acknowledges a Spirit/matter continuum, water, bread, and wine are both rite and reality. Thus the metaphor is more than analogy. It portrays both the objective rite and the subjective/spiritual effect of a sacramental reality.

Gal. 4:6–7

How is one to assess the admission that Gal. 4:6f. "provides strong support for Pentecostal theology."[26] The issue is set in perspective with a question, "What does Paul mean when he says, 'Because you are sons, God has sent the Spirit of his son into your hearts.'"[27] Dunn concludes that it is another conversion-initiation context "in which the metaphors used build up to the culminating thought of the reception of the Spirit, and the correlative concepts of sonship and inheritance."[28]

The verse begins with a ὅτι clause which may introduce either a logical or a chronological sequence in Paul's thought. The conversion-initiation thesis must opt for the logical rather than the chronological. However, the use of ὅτι is not of itself conclusive evidence for either interpretation. It may be recitative, declarative, or causal.[29] Since it does not here introduce a direct quotation (recitative ὅτι), the choice is between the declarative and the causal senses. Dunn is aware of this, of course, but concludes that "even if we take ὅτι = 'because' the more plausible [?] interpretation is that 4.6 refers to the gift of the Spirit at conversion-initiation."[30] It must be noted, however, that this conclusion is not dictated by the grammar of the passage, but by the underlying assumptions of the conversion-initiation thesis.

The causal sense of ὅτι may just as well support the chronological interpretation that the Galatians received the Spirit of the Son because they were already sons by adoption.

The chronological (Pentecostal) understanding is faulted because it does not deal satisfactorily with two of Paul's metaphors, "of Christians as heirs before their conversion," and "the slavery metaphor."[31] He is correct in saying that "Paul combines two metaphors which do not really cohere."[32] The hermeneutical task here is to discover how, individually and collectively, they bear on the question at hand.

Who then are the Christians that are "heirs before their conversion?" In *what* sense may they be called "heirs before their conversion?" The context supplies the answer to both questions. They were "those who were under the law" whom Christ came to redeem (Gal. 4:5). In his polemic against the Judaizers in Galatia, Paul addressed Jewish converts who were in danger of being seduced into legalism. Under the OT economy, "to them belong sonship, the glory, the covenants, the giving of the law, the worship, and the promises" (Rom. 9:4). Under the older covenant, their sonship is a recurrent theme, "Thus says the Lord, Israel is my first-born son" (Ex. 4:22).[33]

In this sense, of prior sonship under the older economy, they may be called "heirs before their conversion." A summary comment by Dunn is consistent with this, for he writes, "Thus the time of adoption is the same as the time when the son and heir comes of age. This entry upon the full rights and experience of sonship is effected by the sending of the Spirit of the Son"[34]—upon those who are *already* sons! This comment accords well with the chronological (Pentecostal) position, for the sending of the Spirit of the Son does not *make* them sons. It marks, rather, the *full* entry *of the sons* and heirs into the full rights and experience of sonship. In the opinion of a Pentecostal, it seems that Dunn has inadvertently conceded an essential point in the Pentecostal hermeneutic.

The slavery metaphor is a bit more complex in its application. There is no evidence that the subject of this metaphor has changed. It is still "those who are under the law," who by the redemption provided by Christ "receive adoption." Dunn's epitome of the metaphor is quite accurate, for he writes, "in the second, it is seen in terms of the slave becoming an *adopted* son. But there is not a clean break between the two metaphors. For the idea of slavery is identified with that of minority."[35]

In the interpretation of the second metaphor, the expression τὴν υἱοθεσίαν, "the adoption," is the *crux interpretum*. The term is a distinctively Pauline one, occurring five times in his epistles.[36] The parallel passage in Rom. 8:15 is especially helpful in interpreting υἱοθεσίαν because of an antithetical parallelism in which it is used. The text reads as follows, "For you did not receive the spirit of slavery (πνεῦμα δουλείας) . . . but you have received the Spirit of sonship (πνεῦμα υἱοθεσίας)." The decisive question here is whether "the spirit of sonship = the Spirit of the Son = the Holy Spirit. If so, it would weigh in favor of the conversion-initiation thesis, that one becomes a son by the gift of the Spirit.

While this is commonly inferred, it does not come to grips with the polarity between "the spirit of slavery" and "the spirit of sonship."

This is an antithetical parallelism. If, therefore, "the spirit of sonship" is personified as "the Spirit of the Son," the parallel metaphor, "the spirit of slavery," must also be personified as "the Spirit of slavery" to preserve the parallelism. But this does not accord well with the context, as illustrated by the RSV translation, "the spirit" (lower case in both places). The NASB gives an even more literal rendering of the Greek text by translating "a spirit," lower case in both members of the parallelism.

If "the spirit of slavery" is the animating, or vital principle, that characterizes slavery, then by parity of reasoning, "the spirit of sonship" is the animating, or vital principle that characterizes sonship. It may be concluded then that "a spirit of adoption as sons" precedes and prepares the way for the reception of the Spirit of the Son.

We must reject, therefore, the equation that "the time of adoption" = "the time when the son and heir comes of age" = "the sending of the Spirit of the Son"[37] = the (Lukan) gift of the Holy Spirit. Their adoption as sons (4:5) preceded their reception of the Spirit of His Son (4:6). Thus the Pentecostal may claim Gal. 4:4ff. as "strong support" for his Pentecostal theology.

Notes

[1] Dunn, op. cit., pp. 103–115.
[2] Ibid., p. 103.
[3] Ibid.
[4] Ibid.
[5] Ibid., p. 104.
[6] Ibid.
[7] Ibid.
[8] Ibid.
[9] Ibid.
[10] Ibid., italics added.
[11] Ibid., p. 105.
[12] Ibid.
[13] Ibid., p. 106.
[14] Ibid.
[15] Ibid.
[16] Ibid.
[17] Ibid., p. 107, italics added.
[18] Ibid., italics added.
[19] Ibid.
[20] Ibid.
[21] Ibid., p. 109.
[22] Ibid., p. 108.

[23]Ibid.
[24]Ibid., p. 109.
[25]Ibid., p. 112.
[26]Ibid., p. 113.
[27]Ibid.
[28]Ibid., p. 115.
[29]A. T. Robertson and W. Hersey Davis, *A New Short Grammar of the New Testament* (New York: Harper & Brothers, 1933), p. 310.
[30]Dunn, op. cit., p. 114.
[31]Ibid.
[32]Ibid.
[33]Cf. Deut. 14:1; Jer. 31:9; Hosea 11:1.
[34]Dunn, op. cit., p. 114.
[35]Ibid.
[36]Rom. 8:15, 23; 9:4; Gal. 4:5; Eph. 1:5.
[37]Dunn, op. cit., p. 114.

Chapter 10

The Corinthian Epistles

To what extent may one find conversion-initiation contexts in the Corinthian epistles? This chapter will focus on the answers provided in "The Corinthian Epistles."[1]

I Cor. 1:4–9

In this passage, Paul speaks in general terms of important elements in the Christian experience of the Corinthians. Two are especially significant for the present discussion, namely, conversion (vv. 4, 9), and (*charismata*) spiritual gifts, (v. 7). Conversion is alluded to in the χάρις of v. 4, "the work of grace in conversion,"[2] and again in the ἐκλήθητε of v. 9, "called into the fellowship of his Son." Two of the charismata (v. 7) are referred to specifically, that is, λόγος and γνῶσις, *word* and *knowledge*. The latter appear again in the context of the πνευματικῶν, "spirituals," in I Cor. 12:1ff.

The Pentecostal must regard it as a counsel of expediency to claim, as Dunn does, that "Here conversion is thought of in terms of a gift of grace, an enriching with spiritual gifts."[3] This provides the occasion to press again the point made earlier. If spiritual gifts are simply an enriching of the conversion-initiation experience, is conversion-initiation complete without them? Given the logic of the conversion-initiation paradigm, should it not read, repentance, faith, water baptism, the gift of the Spirit, *and* the (Pentecostal) charisms of the Spirit?

However, the juxtaposition of *conversion* and *spiritual gifts* in I Cor. 1:4–9 does not thereby validate the conversion-initiation exegesis. As a matter of record, the charisms of λόγος and γνῶσις appear again in I Cor. 12:8, which is *not* a conversion context. Along with the other charisms listed in the context, they represent the supernatural manifestations of the Spirit in the worship and witness of the Christian community. Yet without any mention of *either* the Spirit *or* baptism,[4] I Cor. 1:4–9 is claimed as evidence for the conversion-initiation hypothesis. To the Pentecostal this is an arbitrary application of the paradigm without justification from the context itself.

On the other hand, with the paradigm of conversion and subsequent baptism in the Spirit provided by Acts, the Pentecostal may legitimately, and with greater cogency, see in the passage conversion with its attendant new birth and a subsequent baptism in the Spirit, evidenced by the Spirit's gifts. It is, in fact, the specific mention of χαρίσματα in the context that lends support to the Pentecostal thesis.

I Cor. 1:10–17

Initially this critique began as a response to the author's anti-Pentecostal challenge. It soon became apparent, however, that both his anti-Pentecostalism and his antisacramentalism shared the same theological root system. As a consequence, a critique of his pneumatology makes a response to his antisacramentalism inevitable.

Such a response is called for in answer to his discussion of baptism in I Cor. 1:10–17. The crux of the passage is v. 17, "For Christ did not send me to baptize but to preach the gospel." Dunn remarks that "v. 17 sets water-baptism in antithesis with that through which the Spirit works to effect salvation."[5] However, the context does not support a claim of "antithesis" between baptism and preaching. There is an antithesis in the passage, but it is not between baptism per se and the preaching of the gospel. The antithesis is between the sectarian spirit that had coalesced around prominent teachers and the unity of the Church. Baptism is derogated only to the degree that it identifies believers with party leaders. Paul does not relegate baptism itself to a place of relative unimportance. What he does deprecate is the partisan strife whereby baptism has been demeaned to sectarian ends among the Corinthians. One may not be able to demonstrate from this text that baptism is a sacrament, but then neither can it be demonstrated that it occupies a place of inferiority in Paul's theology.

The derogation of baptism goes a long step further when he says, "when baptism was abused and its role misunderstood, he turned away from it and put its function in proper perspective by highlighting that which really matters in the ministering and receiving of salvation."[6] "Baptism abused . . . its role misunderstood, he [Paul] turned away from it;"—the perceptive reader will be aware that these are a priori assumptions. It accords better with what we perceive to be the intention of the text to say, "Baptism is not disparaged by this, but baptism presupposes that the great charge to preach the Gospel has been fulfilled."[7]

The fact that Paul baptized only Crispus, Gaius, and the household of Stephanas does not support the contention that "he turned away" from baptism. Rather, his conduct relative to baptism in Corinth seems to have been in accord with established apostolic precedent. For example, neither Jesus (John 4:1, 2) nor Peter (Acts 10:48) seems to have baptized personally. In these instances, it is the disciples of each who perform the actual rite.

No more do his words in v. 17, "For Christ did not send me to baptize but to preach the gospel," detract from the significance of baptism. Paul's words must be heard in their Corinthian context. Given the schismatic spirit that prevailed in Corinth (marriage versus celibacy, meats sacrificed to idols, debauchery at the Eucharist, denial of the resurrection, all figured in the sectarian strife there), could baptism escape unscathed? In arriving at a judgment on baptism in this context, it would be well to remember that, despite debauchery at the Eucharist, Paul did not turn away from it. Thus the sectarian spirit in Corinth renders no negative judgment against the intrinsic worth of baptism. The abuse of a doctrine (or sacrament) does not dictate its value.

The terms of Paul's apostolic commission to preach the gospel rather than to baptize "should not be pushed to mean that Paul felt that baptism was of secondary importance and more or less dispensable."[8] If, as Dunn says, "the verse comes at one extreme of Paul's doctrine of baptism,"[9] then the antisacramental statements made above need to be balanced by Paul's other statements relative to baptism, for example, Rom. 6:3ff.

I Cor. 6:11

That the majority of commentators regard I Cor. 6:11 as a baptismal text is acknowledged by Dunn, but he counters by saying, "But in fact Paul is not talking about baptism at all—he speaks rather of the great spiritual transformation of conversion."[10]

Once again, it may be objected that the exegesis of the verse does not support this contention. The verb ἀπολούω is used only twice in the NT, here and in Acts 22:16. In Acts 22:16, it is used in an unmistakable baptismal text, "Rise and be baptized, and wash away (ἀπόλουσαι) your sins"—and clearly this is its sense in the context of the Corinthian passage. In the absence of any other parallel, its use in Acts 22:16 provides strong presumptive support for the baptismal significance of ἀπολούω in I Cor. 6:11.

In addition, it may be argued that the phrase, "in the name of the Lord Jesus Christ," in conjunction with ἀπολούω, strengthens the baptismal sense of the text.[11] Again Dunn acknowledges as much, but he tries to blunt the effect of the admission by adding, "But in the Synoptics and Acts similar phrases are mostly used in connection with healings and exorcisms."[12] But this is entirely irrelevant to the case in point. It is baptism that is alluded to in the context. Healings and exorcisms are not even suggested in this context.

The question at issue is this. What does the phrase ἀπολού-σασθε . . . ἐν τῷ ὀνόματι, "you were washed . . . in the name," mean in this context? Dunn concludes that "what Paul is really thinking of in his use of the phrase ἐν τῷ ὀνόματι . . . is not the rite of baptism."[13] However, as we have shown above, the allusion in ἀπολούω is to baptism, and it is consistent with Paul's doctrine of baptism to see in this use of the clause an allusion to the believer's mystical union with Christ in baptism (cf. Rom. 6:3ff.).

As crucial for his interpretation, Dunn appeals to the context. He argues that the interpretation of the verb ἀπολούω, "cannot be divorced from the preceding list of vices."[14] And we can agree without accepting his conclusions. He adds that since these are of a moral and spiritual nature:

Whatever washes them away is a cleansing of the heart and conscience . . . ἀπολούσασθε, like ἡγιάσθητε and ἐδικαιώθητε, therefore, deals primarily with matters of the heart and spiritual relationships and does not have its first reference to baptism.[15]

However, the three verbs, *washed, sanctified,* and *justified* are to be read in series, as the thrice repeated ἀλλά before each verb indicates. Read in series with the two following verbs, ἀπελούσασθε = baptism *is* included in "the process by which the Corinthians were changed."[16] We may conclude, therefore, that the context offers no grammatical support for the exclusion of baptism from "cleansing of the heart and conscience."

Thus the judgments expressed in support of the conversion-initiation thesis are not primarily of an exegetical nature but are logical constructs predicated upon the Spirit/matter dichotomy of the antisacramentalist. Sooner or later, it is to be hoped, even the theologian must acknowledge that God is no longer boxed in by the arbitrary Spirit/matter categories of an outmoded physics. From an experiential point of view, an experience with the charismata of the Holy Spirit makes a Spirit/matter dichotomy untenable for the Pentecostal. For the Pentecostal who reflects upon his experience, a Spirit/matter (i.e., energy/matter) continuum offers little credibility to an antisacramental metaphysics.

I Cor. 6:14–20

Even though it is acknowledged that this is not a conversion-initiation text, [17] it is, nonetheless, concluded that "6.17 therefore shows beyond dispute that the indwelling Spirit is inseparable from union with Christ, and that the gift of the Spirit is what effects this union."[18] The Pentecostal would agree that "the indwelling Spirit is inseparable from union with Christ" and that this is experienced at conversion in the new birth. But he would insist that this is *not* to be identified with the gift of the Spirit = the baptism in/filling with the Spirit for power-in-mission.

I Cor. 10:1–5

While acknowledging that the "majority of commentators refer 10.1–5 directly to the Christian sacrament,"[19] Dunn constructs a detailed rationale for rejecting this view. Specifically, he says of the πνευματικὸν βρῶμα/πόμα, *spiritual food/drink*, in vv. 3 and 4 that

Paul is not saying that the Israelites partook of spiritual sustenance, nor that the manna and water were any more than manna and water. He is simply using the manna and water . . . as an illustration of the spiritual sustenance Christians receive from Christ, their living Head.[20]

It may be objected that this conclusion destroys the symmetry of Paul's parallelism, for "all ate the same *supernatural* food and drank the same *supernatural* drink" (RSV).

Going a step further, Dunn adds:

The immediate reference of the allegory is not to the elements of the Lord's Supper, for then the equation would have been drawn between the βρῶμα and the πόμα on the one hand and the body and blood of Christ on the other.[21]

Anticipating a little, this is precisely the equation we intend to demonstrate contextually, for it is Paul's allusion "to the manna . . . as *spiritual food* and water from the rock as *spiritual drink*, which suggest the eating and drinking of the Lord's Supper (as becomes evident from 10:16–22)."[22]

The interpretation adopted by Dunn here is further compromised by a methodological weakness. In the first place, vv. 1–5 is too restricted a segment of the context to determine clearly the intention of the passage. Second, and closely related to the first, the primary theme of the larger

context is a discussion of, and warning against, idolatry beginning with
8:1ff., "Now concerning food offered to idols," and continuing
through 11.1ff. In this regard note especially 10:31 in relation to 8:1,
"So whether you eat or drink."

The immediate context of 10:1–5 extends at least to 10:22. In the
light of his warning against the perils of idolatry, a chiasmus in Paul's
thought serves to clarify the peril in which "food offered to idols" (8:1)
placed the Corinthians. It may be illustrated as follows.

Sacramental Meal (Israel)	Idolatry (Israel)
"Our fathers . . . all ate the same supernatural food [manna] and all drank the same supernatural drink . . . from the supernatural Rock . . . and the Rock was Christ" (vv. 1, 3, 4).	"Do not be idolaters as some of them were; as it is written, 'The people sat down to eat and drink and rose up to dance'" [i.e., before the golden calf; cf. Ex. 32:6] (v. 7).
Idolatry (Corinthians)	**Sacramental Meal (Corinthians)**
"Therefore, my beloved, shun the worship of idols (v. 14) (You cannot drink the cup of the Lord and the cup of demons" v. 21).	"The cup of blessing which we bless, is it not a participation in the blood of Christ? The bread which we break, is it not a participation in the body of Christ" (v. 16).

Paul's exegetical method here is akin to Jewish midrash in which OT
events are seen to prefigure NT parallels. The intention of the comparison is to warn the Corinthians against idolatry and its consequences.
Participation in the Christian Eucharist is totally incompatible with "eucharistic" fellowship in the stuff of pagan "sacraments."

As the chiastic structure above illustrates, the Israelites ate
πνευματικὸν (*supernatural*, RSV) βρῶμα, and drank πνευματικὸν
(*supernatural*, RSV) πόμα. They shared a sacramental fellowship in
the supernaturally provided manna and water from the Rock. Neverthe-

less, they apostatized by sharing a "sacramental" communion with the demonic powers represented in the golden calf.

The warning is clear to the Corinthians. They cannot participate in the Christian Eucharist, which is a participation in the body and blood of Jesus, and then drink the "sacramental" cup of idol worship. As in the experience of ancient Israel, so here the danger of apostasy is implicit. One may perhaps wonder to what degree an echo of this is heard in Paul's admonition, "Whoever, therefore, eats the bread or drinks the cup of the Lord in an unworthy manner will be guilty of profaning the body and blood of the Lord" (I Cor. 11:27). In passing, it is important to note again that the "body *and blood* of the Lord" is hardly a figure of the Church.

Excursus on the Lord's Supper as Sacrament

It is at this point that a substantive question calls for an answer. What does Dunn mean here by a sacrament? He responds by saying, "*our* literal, physical immersion and eating of bread and wine are sacraments because they point to our redemption in Christ."[23] One could substitute the words symbol or ordinance here without materially altering the sense of this definition. But if water, wine, and bread merely "point to our redemption in Christ," then Christ is not "present" in His Eucharistic body and blood, and one may legitimately question the appropriateness of calling it a sacrament.

The eucharistic question revolves around the words of institution, "this is my body . . . this cup is the new covenant in my blood" (I Cor. 11:24, 25). From the standpoint of the Greek text, this presents a grammatical problem. Does the *neuter* demonstrative τοῦτο, *this*, refer to the *masculine* noun ἄρτον, *bread*, e.g., "This (bread) is my body?" On the side of the sacramental view, it may be said that even though ἄρτον is masculine (one would expect the adjective to agree with its noun in gender), it seems reasonably clear that the adjective has assimilated to the neuter predicate nominative (τὸ σῶμα, "body") with which it is linked grammatically, e.g., τοῦτο μού ἐστιν τὸ σῶμα, "this (bread) is my body." Then too, the neuter τοῦτο τὸ ποτήριον, "this cup" (v. 25), refers unquestionably to the wine of the sacrament. Consequently, the parallelism between bread and wine would require that we understand that τοῦτο, even though neuter, does refer to ἄρτον, "bread," in v. 24.

A more pragmatic question is implicit in v. 27, "Whoever, therefore, eats the bread or drinks the cup of the Lord [contrast with "the cup of demons," 10:21] in an unworthy manner will be guilty of profaning the body and blood of the Lord." In support of a symbolic interpretation of the passage, it is frequently observed that "discerning the body" (v. 29) is a metaphor of the body of Christ, that is the Church and, consequently, determines the meaning of "body" in the context. However, as pointed out above, "body *and blood*" (v. 27) is not a metaphor of the Church. The reference is clearly to the Eucharistic elements, and contextual exegesis dictates that v. 29 be read in sequence with v. 27.

The question that this verse poses, and which the symbolic interpretation does not answer satisfactorily, is this. How may one "be guilty of profaning the body and blood of the Lord" simply by eating the bread and drinking the cup "in an unworthy manner," *unless* the Eucharistic bread and wine truly are (in a modality *not propositionally defined*) "the body and blood of the Lord?" If, for the sake of argument, the Eucharistic bread and wine are regarded as less than a sacrament, they are certainly more than metaphysical symbols whose sole function "is only to symbolize the union of the intellect with God and Christ."[24]

To one less sophisticated (theologically), the pragmatic question may well be a simplistic, but, nonetheless, biblical observation. If Jesus, in the days of His flesh, turned water into wine at the marriage feast in Cana (John 2:9), is He now unable to turn bread and wine into his body and blood at the Eucharistic feast of His Church?

I Cor. 12:13

The discussion of the conversion-initiation thesis, insofar as it relates to the Corinthian epistles of Paul, focuses primarily upon I Cor. 12:13, "For by [ἐν–*in*] one Spirit we were all baptized into one body (εἰς ἕν σῶμα ἐβαπτίσθημεν). . . . and all were made to drink of one Spirit (ἕν πνεῦμα ἐποτίσθημεν)." Not only is this verse "crucial for the Pentecostal,"[25] conversely, it is crucial for the conversion-initiation hypothesis. It is the only verse in Paul's epistles that speaks unambiguously of a baptism in the Holy Spirit.[26] We must, however, dissent from Dunn's conclusion that "once the initiatory and incorporative significance of the metaphor is grasped, the Pentecostal arguments fall to the ground."[27] Two questions must be dealt with before the impasse can be resolved, (1) the translation of the preposition ἐν and (2) the exegesis of the two verbs, ἐβαπτίσθημεν, "we were baptized," and ἐποτίσθημεν, "we were made to drink."

In the translation of the preposition ἐν, the versions are divided between the instrumental "by" and the locative "in." In favor of the former, it may be noted that ἐν with πνεῦμα is used once in v. 3 and twice in v. 9, where the instrumental "by" best serves the intention of the passage. This provides a contextual precedent favoring the instrumental "by" in I Cor. 12:13, that is, *"by* one Spirit." That is to say, the Spirit is the one who does the baptizing.

Against this interpretation, it has been urged that making the Spirit the baptizer deprives the context of an element in which the baptism takes place. The force of this objection is blunted, however, if one assumes that an allusion to water baptism is implied in ἐβαπτίσθημεν. Such an assumption is in itself (1) consistent with Paul's use of βαπτίζω and (2) with the initiatory role of water baptism. In this scenario, the convert is initiated "into (εἰς) the one body" through water baptism, which from the spiritual standpoint is administered *by* the Spirit. On this interpretation, it is obvious that the conversion-initiation paradigm must forfeit a text "crucial" to its theological survival.

On the other hand, the locative "in" best suits the conversion-initiation hypothesis for obvious reasons. If one is initiated "into the one body" by a baptism *in* the Spirit, does this not prove the main contention of the conversion-initiation theory, namely, that the baptism in the Spirit is primarily initiatory?

The conclusion is too facile and rests upon the unproven assumption that Paul and Luke use the phrase, baptism in the Spirit, univocally. Another objection to it is the fact that making the Spirit the element in which the believer is baptized leaves the rite without an administrator. In the Lukan contexts, Jesus is always the baptizer.

It has been urged in favor of this view that the phrase "to baptize *in* the Holy Spirit" occurs seven times in the NT.[28] Vis-à-vis the Corinthian passage, this constitutes a ratio of six to one. It would appear then that numerically this provides an overwhelming precedent in favor of the locative "in one Spirit" (12:13). Such a methodology is, however, fallacious since the six non-Pauline references are all directly related to the one utterance of John the Baptist.[29] The comparison is, therefore, in the nature of a one to one ratio.

What now of the exegesis of the text? Given the instrumental interpretation of ἐν above, the passage poses no problem for the Pentecostal. On the one hand, it must be made clear that even assuming the locative, "in one Spirit," the Pentecostal arguments do not "fall to the ground."

Three different interpretations have been proposed for the verse. (1) Both metaphors refer to baptism, but this assumes a *synonymous* parallelism between the images, "we were baptized" and "we were made to drink." (It is my own view that the parallelism is not *synonymous;* it is *synthetic* in which the second metaphor supplements the first.) (2) The first figure refers to baptism as an initiatory rite, the second to "the outpouring of spiritual gifts after baptism."[30] (3) The first half of the verse is a reference to baptism, the second is a reference to the Eucharist."[31] The first is essentially the conversion-initiation view; the second is, with some nuancing of terms, compatible with the Pentecostal thesis.

In the conversion-initiation scenario, if both figures are regarded as a synonymous parallelism, then a curious mixed-metaphor results. Since baptism in one Spirit is "into" (εἰς) one body, then by parity of reasoning, drinking of one Spirit must also initiate one "into" the one body. On second thought, the imagery of drinking one's way into the body is more than a curious mixing of metaphors.

Dunn cuts the Gordian knot here by repudiating the translation of ποτίζειν, "to drink," in favor of the meaning "to pour." He supports this translation by an examination of the uses of ποτίζω in the passive in biblical (LXX) Greek. Of the three OT occurrences noted, the subject of two of them is the land. In the third example, the verb is used with πνεῦμα (Is. 29:10). Here Dunn makes a point that "this is the only time that ποτίζειν is used to translate *nāsak*, but *nāsak* never has any other sense than 'to pour out.'"[32] It is this exegesis of *nāsak* = ποτίζω that provides the basis for his conclusion:

Conversion, for Paul and the Corinthians, was an experience of the Spirit which was like the outpouring of a sudden flood or rainstorm on a parched ground, and which made their lives like a well-watered garden."[33]

The error in this exegesis is obvious. The *subject* of the verb ἐποτίσθημεν is not the Spirit; it is the first common plural pronoun *we*, i.e., the Christian community in Corinth with which Paul associates himself. Therefore, the contention that *the Spirit* is poured out is an unacceptable wrenching of the metaphor. If the meaning "to pour out" is substituted for "to drink," the translation must then be, "we (not the Spirit) were poured out." Obviously, this is *not* what the text is saying. Furthermore, the use of the masculine plural adjective πάντες, "all" modifying the subject "we" precludes any notion that the Spirit (πνεῦμα is neuter) is here "poured out." The translation, "poured out," must be rejected as an exotic excursus that misrepresents the intentionality of the text. On the other hand, and consistent with the intent of the text is the translation *"we have all been made to drink* (or been imbued with) *the same Spirit."*[34]

Helen Barrett Montgomery's paraphrase of Eph. 5:18 suggests an insight into the import of Paul's metaphor in I Cor. 12:13. She translated the text thus, "Do not be drunk with wine . . . but drink deep in the Spirit."[35] Her paraphrase of the Greek πληροῦσθε as "drink deep," rather than the more literal "be filled," is defensible as a parallelism with μεθύσκεσθε, "(do not) be drunken."

In the context of the parallelism, how does one become drunken? By drinking wine to excess. How is one filled with the Spirit? By "drink(ing) deep in the Spirit." Thus "drink deep in the Spirit" parallels the figure "be filled with the Spirit." The parallelism of metaphors may well be an autobiographical allusion to Paul's own experience of being filled with the Spirit (Acts 9:17) as "drinking (deep) of one Spirit" (I Cor. 12:13). The parallelism of metaphors, in the light of Paul's own experience, suggests that fullness of the Spirit, rather than conversion-initiation, is the intent of ἐποτίσθημεν in I Cor. 12:13.

Thus, according to this scripting of the text, εἰς ἕν σῶμα ἐβαπτίσθημεν, "we were baptized into one body," is initiatory, while ἐν πνεῦμα ἐποτίσθημεν, "we were made to drink of one Spirit" is another metaphor for the filling with/baptism in/gift of the Holy Spirit for power-in-mission. In response, therefore, to Dunn's "initiatory and incorporative significance" of the metaphors, we would reply that this is too arbitrary a harmonization of the figures. The verbs here describe two distinct relationships of the Christian to the Holy Spirit. In the one, the Spirit is the medium in which the convert is immersed into the body of Christ. The analogy is with water baptism. However, to say that "for Paul βαπτίζειν has only two meanings . . . either the water-rite . . . or the spiritual transformation . . . the metaphor [does not] include the ritual act within itself"[36] is too draconian a judgment. What has happened to the paradigm of conversion-initiation contexts "whatever elements are present or absent?"[37] If the ritual act is excluded, is this still claimed as a conversion-initiation context?

In summary, we are saying that in interpreting the baptismal metaphor, the phrase εἰς ἕν σῶμα, *into one body,* weighs in favor of Christian initiation. However, this is not the whole of the context, and contextual as well as hermeneutical considerations argue for an *equivocal* rather than a *univocal* sense in which baptism in the Spirit is to be understood here. The phrase cannot be conflated univocally into one sense in the NT. Contextual considerations, as these reflect the theology and literary style of the several authors, must be consulted. (The Lukan sense of the metaphor is not definitive of the Pauline usage.) The conversion-initiation hypothesis receives no support then whether one opts for either the locative or the instrumental sense of ἐν, in/by one Spirit, in I Cor. 12:13.

In the context, the use of the verb ἐποτίσθημεν, "we were made to drink," describes metaphorically a second relationship of the believer to the Holy Spirit that is not identical to the first. An "initiative and incorporative significance" cannot, therefore, be imposed *univocally* upon both figures. As suggested above, analogies with Eph. 5:18 evoke the Pentecostal imagery of filling with/baptism in the Spirit for power-in-mission. The paraphrase of Eph. 5:18 bespeaks the continuous filling (empowerment) with the Spirit of those baptized into the one body. A Pentecostal theology would, therefore, reject the claim that ἐποτίσθημεν is a conversion-initiation metaphor.

Parenthetically, the "all" in I Cor. 12:13 need not give one pause. In the apostolic age, the baptism in the Spirit, in a Pentecostal sense, was the norm.[38] A dichotomy between the "haves" and the "have nots" is not a fact of Scripture. It is, however, a datum of current Church life. By reading conversion-initiation as the norm of apostolic experience, the apparent dichotomy in contemporary Christian experience is resolved. But, to exacerbate the dichotomy by insisting that a Pentecostal baptism in the Spirit, subsequent to conversion, is still the norm for Christian spirituality, is to invite the charge of elitism, a staple in the modern anti-Pentecostal polemic.

Furthermore, Paul's charge that they were carnal and babes in Christ does not contradict their "all" having experienced a Pentecostal baptism in the Spirit. The Pentecostal baptism in the Spirit is for power-in-mission. It is not instant maturity—contrary to the assumptions of an anti-Pentecostal rhetoric. Paul makes it clear that the Corinthians are carnal and spiritually immature because of their schismatic spirit (I Cor. 1:11f., 3:11f.), while at the same time acknowledging that they did not lack any spiritual gift (I Cor. 1:6). The manifestations of the Spirit's charisms are neither evidence of, nor contingent upon, spiritual maturity. Partisan views of sanctification have obscured this fact.

II Cor. 1:21

Is the context of II Cor. 1.21f. "a description either of baptism or the baptismal experience, of Confirmation or a post-baptismal experience, or a combination of these?"[39] Having raised the question, Dunn responds that "the proper interpretation is of the experience of the Spirit in conversion-initiation."[40] A detailed response to his exposition of the passage is unnecessary. A single example will suffice to demonstrate its fallacy.

Focusing on the expression καὶ χρίσας ἡμᾶς, he says "Since χρίω elsewhere in the NT is used only of Jesus, Paul's choice of it here is no accident but a deliberate play on words—εἰς Χριστὸν καὶ χρίσας. Paul is almost certainly thinking of Jesus' anointing with the Spirit at Jordan (Luke 4.1–8; Acts 4.27; 10.38)."[41] With the statement that "χρίω elsewhere in the NT is used only of Jesus," there is no disagreement. However, the subsequent inference drawn from it is logically incoherent, for he says, "The anointing of God which made Jesus the Christ is the same as the anointing of God which makes men Christians."[42] This is a non sequitur. The comparision of a functional category (Christ = Messiah) with an ontological category (Christian = sons of God) is a category mistake. The anointing of Jesus at Jordan did not make Him the Son of God. He is the Son of God by virtue of His Incarnation. The anointing (ἔχρισεν) that made Jesus "the Christ" was an empowerment (δυνάμει) for His Messianic ministry (Acts 10:38).

If, therefore, the anointing is *the same* in both cases, then the anointing of the Corinthians did not make them the sons of God either. Their chrismation, like the chrismation of Jesus, was an empowerment for mission.

On the basis of the foregoing evidence, it may be concluded that the Corinthian epistles of Paul offer no substantive support to the conversion-initiation hypothesis.

Notes

[1]Dunn, op. cit., pp. 116–138.
[2]Bauer, Arndt, Gingrich.
[3]Dunn, op. cit., p. 116.
[4]Ibid., p. 117.
[5]Ibid., p. 119.
[6]Ibid.
[7]Archibald Robertson and Alfred Plummer, *A Critical and Exegetical Commentary on the First Epistle of St. Paul to the Corinthians*, The International Critical Commentary (1911; rpt. Edinburgh: T. & T. Clark, 1963), p. 15.
[8]William F. Orr and James Arthur Walther, *I Corinthians, A New Translation*, The Anchor Bible (New York: Doubleday & Company, Inc., 1976), p. 151.
[9]Dunn, op. cit., p. 120.
[10]Ibid., p. 121.
[11]Cf. Acts 2:38; 10:48; 8:16; 19:5.

[12]Dunn, op. cit., p. 121.
[13]Ibid., p. 122.
[14]Ibid., p. 121.
[15]Ibid.
[16]Orr and Walther, op. cit., p. 201.
[17]Dunn, op. cit., p. 123.
[18]Ibid., p. 124.
[19]Ibid., p. 124, n. 25.
[20]Ibid., p. 125.
[21]Ibid.
[22]Orr and Walther, op. cit., p. 247.
[23]Dunn, op. cit., p. 127.
[24]John Meyendorff, *Byzantine Theology* (New York: Fordham University Press, 1974), p. 28.
[25]Dunn, op. cit., p. 127.
[26]Ibid.
[27]Ibid., p. 129.
[28]Cf. Matt. 3:11; Mark 1:8; Luke 3:16; John 1:33; Acts 1:5; 11:16; I Cor. 12:13.
[29]Robert W. Graves in private correspondence.
[30]Robertson and Plummer, op. cit., p 272.
[31]Ibid.
[32]Dunn, op. cit., p. 131.
[33]Ibid.
[34]Bauer, Arndt, Gingrich.
[35]Centenary Translation of the New Testament.
[36]Dunn, op. cit., p. 130.
[37]Ibid., p. 104.
[38]Cf. Acts 2:4; 4:31; 8:17; 10:44; 19:6.
[39]Dunn, op. cit., p. 131.
[40]Ibid.
[41]Ibid., p. 133.
[42]Ibid.

Chapter 11

The Epistle to Rome

Does Paul's epistle to the Romans provide the anticipated "fuller insight"[1] on the subject of conversion-initiation? The significant arguments in support of this assumption will be examined in this chapter.

Rom. 5:5

The discussion of Rom. 5:5 centers on Paul's words, "God's love has been poured into our hearts through the Holy Spirit which has been given to us." Singling out the word ἐκκέχυται, Dunn remarks:

ἐκκέχυται, when connected with the Spirit vividly recalls Pentecost. As the disciples began their Christian lives at Pentecost with the outpouring of Christ's Spirit and God's love in their hearts, so did each one begin his Christian life in these early days of Christianity. There is no question of distinguishing the initial experience of God's love, of which the perfect ἐκκέχυται speaks, from the initial gift of the Holy Spirit. For Paul they are one. Christian conversion is nothing other than a being seized and overwhelmed by the love of God in the person of the Holy Spirit.[2]

Two questions clamor for an answer at this point. (1) Did the disciples really begin "their Christian lives at Pentecost?" We have already responded to and rejected this claim. In his discussion of "The Johannine Pentecost?" Dunn concedes that the disciples were born again on the resurrection day (John 20:22). They, therefore, "began their Christian lives" on the resurrection day, and this is in flat contradiction to the assertion above that "the disciples began their Christian lives at Pentecost." (2) Is it legitimate, from a methodological point of view, to conflate "the outpouring of Christ's Spirit *and* God's love" into a compound subject of the verb ἐκκέχυται? This does violence to the syntax of the text. In 5:5 it is God's love that has been poured into our hearts through (διά) the Holy Spirit. The Holy Spirit is the originator of the action.[3]

Granted, the verb ἐκχέω, "pour out," does occur in the Pentecost context, but it is more than a moot question, indeed, whether or not a verbal correspondence between Acts 2:33 and Rom. 5:5 is sufficient to establish a common theme. In Acts 2:33, Jesus is the *agent* through whom the Holy Spirit is poured out upon His disciples. In Rom 5:5, the Holy Spirit is the *agent* through whom the love of God is poured into our hearts.

The subject of ἐκκέχυται in Rom. 5:5 is ἡ ἀγάπη τοῦ θεοῦ, "the love of God," not πνεύματος ἁγίου, "the Holy Spirit." Therefore, to conflate "the outpouring of Christ's Spirit *and* God's love" into a compound subject of the verb is to theologize a conclusion at the expense of the syntax. This is simply another category mistake.

The verb ἐκκέχυται is perfect, indicative, passive. For contextual reasons, this is interpreted herewith as a present perfect in which the action is both punctiliar and linear. Thus the text is saying that the love of God *has been* poured into our hearts and *continues* to flood our hearts. On the other hand, the Holy Spirit is here qualified attributively by the articular participial phrase τοῦ δοθέντος ἡμῖν, "the one given to us." As an aorist tense, δοθέντος is punctiliar in action. Thus the text is saying that the Holy Spirit was given to us—without reference to time, place, or attendant circumstances—and He in turn has poured into our hearts the love of God which continues to fill our hearts. It is this abiding presence of the love of God that sustains the Christian in tribulation (v. 3).

If the context "vividly recalls Pentecost," then it is important to recall also the incompatibility of the conversion-initiation schema with the events of Pentecost and, by parity of reasoning, the incompatibility of Rom. 5:5 with the conversion-initiation paradigm.

The word ἐκχέω occurs in the context of Peter's proclamation, "And having received from the Father the promise of the Holy Spirit, he has poured out this which you see and hear" (Acts 2:33). The object of ἐκχέω in this text is τοῦτο, expanded to τοῦτο τὸ δῶρον in a variant reading, which "gives the proper sense of τοῦτο."[4] Thus the gift of the Spirit in His charismatic manifestations is the object of ἐκχέω in the Pentecost narrative. There is no reference here to the love of God being poured out. In Rom. 5:5, there is no reference to the Spirit being poured out.

From the Pentecostal point of view, the choice is clear. If the analogue of Rom. 5:5 is Pentecost, then it is not a conversion-initiation context. If it is claimed for a conversion-initiation context, then it is not the Pentecostal gift of the Holy Spirit.

Rom. 6:1–14

With the exposition of Rom. 6:1–14, the focus of the debate shifts from the Pentecostals to the sacramentalists. The discussion opens with a summary statement, "It is important," says Dunn, "to grasp that the subject of Rom. 6 is not baptism but death to sin and the life which follows it."[5] But it may be objected that this confuses metaphors for message and so misses the central theme of the passage. The theme of the context is the believer's mystical union with Christ. "Death to sin, and the life which follows from it" do not in themselves contain the theme; they are metaphors that illustrate aspects of the theme of union with Christ. It is this motif of union with Christ in which *all* the metaphors in the context cohere.

In Dunn's subsequent explanation, "Baptism affords the first strand of the exposition of this theme."[6] However, having confused the metaphors for the message, his exposition is naturally skewed. The theme *is* union with Christ (in death and in life), and it is in this sense that baptism figures in the subsequent discussion of the context.

Mentioned three times in vv. 3 and 4, it (baptism) drops out after a supposed break in the thought after v. 4. The break after v. 4 is, however, a moot point, for change of metaphor does not necessarily represent a discontinuity in the author's thought. The Christian, having been baptized into (εἰς) Christ, is united with Christ. That σύμφυτοι, "united" (v. 5), is an extension of the metaphor of baptism, "into his death" (v. 3), is clear from its connection with "united with his death" (τοῦ θανάτου αὐτοῦ, v. 5).

The key to the meaning of the passage is, for Dunn, v. 2, "without which the meaning of the passage cannot be unlocked and opened up."[7] It is difficult to see how v. 2 ("How can we who died to sin still live in it") helps the conversion-initiation thesis. It simply raises the question: When did the believer die to sin? Paul's answer is direct and to the point, for "all of us who have been baptized into Christ Jesus were baptized into his death" (v. 3). It may be said then that for Paul baptism into (εἰς) Christ Jesus incorporates one into Christ. Likewise, baptism into (εἰς) His death is union with Him in His death to sin.

The plain sense of the passage is rejected by Dunn. He refutes any organic connection between water baptism and these metaphors. Of the verbal phrase, βαπτίζεσθαι εἰς Χριστὸν Ἰησοῦν, (v. 3), he says, "It is drawn from baptism," but does not "contain within itself the thought of the water-rite."[8] What is meant by this "spiritualizing" of the text is not exactly clear. If the metaphor ("baptized into Christ Jesus") does not contain the thought of water baptism within itself, does water baptism contain the metaphor? The verdict of the context is an affirmative one. If not at baptism, then *when* does the union with Christ occur? And, if not in and through water baptism, then *how* does it take place?

Dunn circumvents the plain sense of the context by claiming that "The first and only concrete reference to water-baptism in Rom. 6 is the phrase διὰ τοῦ βαπτίσματος; this phrase marks an extension of Paul's thought to embrace the water rite."[9] If it is an extension of Paul's thought, does it not simply make explicit what is implicit in the phrase βαπτίζεσθαι εἰς Χριστὸν Ἰησοῦν?

"Buried with him by (water) baptism (διὰ τοῦ βαπτίσματος) into death" (v. 4) is a logical progression in the imagery "baptized (immersed) into his death" (v. 3). This is in turn a logical extension of the figure "baptized into Christ Jesus" (v. 3). Things equal to the same thing are equal to each other. Water baptism does contain all of these metaphors within itself, and apart from the water rite, the metaphors have little meaning in themselves. Dunn's claim that the metaphor(s) do not contain within themselves the thought of the water rite is a distinction without substance.

One may fairly say that in Paul's thought a causal relationship does exist between water baptism and its spiritual significance. Given Dunn's pronounced antisacramental bias, it is surprising indeed that he should make a curious concession in favor of a sacramental viewpoint. He says, for instance, "Verse 4 indicates that the rite of water-baptism not only symbolizes burial with Christ, but also that *it helps in some way to effect it* (διὰ τοῦ βαπτίσματος)."[10] But if God through baptism and by means of baptism "effect[s] the spiritual transformation" then "the ceremony" is substantively more than symbolic, it is sacramental, and Dunn has contradicted himself.

This admission is followed by a disclaimer, offered "with some hesitation,"[11] that what Paul, Luke, and I Peter 3:21 have to say in other contexts negates his concession and alters the thought of Rom. 6. He concludes that

Baptism is best seen here, therefore, as a means and step of commitment to Christ which results in new life. Without renunciation of the old life and commitment to the new, there is no death and no life. Baptism does not effect these, but it can be the vital vehicle of their expression.[12]

On methodological grounds alone, this conclusion falters. It is unacceptable from a hermeneutical and an exegetical standpoint to adjust Paul's understanding of baptism in Rom. 6 to conform to Luke and/or Peter. If (?) a substantive difference does exist between Luke and Peter, on the one hand, and Paul, on the other, then it would be just as valid to make Rom. 6 the lodestone by which Luke and Peter are made to conform to Paul.

Excursus on a Pauline Sacramentalism

At this point, a dichotomy in the conversion-initiation thesis emerges. On the one hand, "God operates 'through' and by means of baptism to effect the spiritual transformation," but on the other hand, "Baptism does not effect these." The problem faced here by the conversion-initiation paradigm is how to retain water baptism as a constitutive element, while, at the same time, denying any sacramental realism associated with it. It is, as already suggested, a conflict between exegesis and a philosophical/theological a priori that assumes a Spirit/matter dichotomy. It is this problem that prompts a reflection on a Pauline sacramentalism.

The sacramental reality of which Paul speaks in Rom. 6 goes far beyond the metaphors used to describe it. The words themselves are simply phenomenological descriptions of the numinous reality they portray. Dunn's concession is a candid, albeit grudging, acknowledgment of the sacramental nature of Paul's argument—"On the testimony of Rom. 6 alone one would be justified in arguing that in Paul's view God operates 'through baptism' and by means of baptism to effect the spiritual transformation which the ceremony symbolizes."[13]

What is at issue in the sacramental/antisacramental debate is a clash of world-views. For Paul, the boundary between the material and the spiritual realms is permeable. He is the "man in Christ . . . caught up to the third heaven," whether in the body or out of the body, he does not know (II Cor. 12:2). The paradox defies definition. This points to the paradoxical nature of all spiritual experience, which is at the center of the debate. When a spiritual truth is reduced to the propositional logic of metaphysical systems, the inherent paradoxes are polarized. Within the context of this polarity, sacramentalism may be (1) affirmed as the recapitulation of an authentic apostolic spirituality, or (2) denied as a departure from the propositional word—hence a corrupting of apostolic doctrine.

This is not meant to deny that Paul's spirituality may be stated propositionally, but we must not be deluded thereby into thinking that we have either understood, much less explained, the numinous dimensions of his experience. There is, after all, a boundary between the phenomenological and the spiritual beyond which the categories of propositional logic do not apply. It is a realm in which experience is knowledge and knowledge is experience. In the presence of the (divine) numinous, the only valid epistemology is adoration. Theology is not theology until it is prayed.

Paul's sacramentalism is just such a spirituality. His is the sacramentalism of mystical union, "baptized into Christ Jesus . . . baptized into (his) death" (Rom. 6:3); "crucified with Christ; it is no longer I who live, but Christ lives in me" (Gal. 2:20). His is the sacramentalism of the mystic and the seer, "Whosoever, therefore, eats the bread or drinks the cup of the Lord in an unworthy manner will be guilty of profaning the body and blood of the Lord" (I Cor. 11:27).

This is not to be construed as an argument for a mechanical or magical effect of baptism. In Paul's thought, Spirit, word, water, faith, and commitment are constitutive elements of the whole.

* * * * * * *

An additional argument to bolster his interpretation of Rom. 6:1–14 is derived from Paul's use of ὁμοίωμα, *likeness* (v. 5). He concludes that

It refers neither to baptism itself nor to the death of Christ itself, but rather to the spiritual transformation which takes place at conversion when we become united with a death to sin precisely like Christ's.[14]

The emphasis here is upon "united with *a death* to sin precisely like Christ's." The question at issue is whether the believer is united in an abstract manner with *a death* like Christ's, or united *with Christ* in His death. The latter is certainly more consistent with Paul's view expressed elsewhere (cf. Gal. 2:20, "I have been *crucified with Christ*"). However, having ruled out this latter understanding, Dunn justifies his conclusion by adding, "Otherwise Paul would simply have said, εἰ γὰρ σύμφυτοι γεγόναμεν τῷ θανάτῳ αὐτοῦ,"[15] "for if we have been united with his death."

Insofar as the grammatical construction of the clause is concerned, the interpretation "a death" is permissible, but it does not comport well with the theme of union with Christ, a union expressed by various metaphors in the context. For example:

(1) we have been baptized "into Christ Jesus" (εἰς Χριστὸν Ἰησοῦν, v. 3);

(2) we were baptized "into his death" (εἰς τὸν θάνατον αὐτοῦ, v. 3);

(3) we were buried "with him" by baptism (αὐτῷ, v. 4);

(4) we have died "with Christ" (σὺν Χριστῷ, v. 8);

(5) we shall also live "with him" (αὐτῷ, v. 8);

(6) alive to God "in Christ Jesus" (ἐν Χριστῷ Ἰησοῦ, v. 11).

The evidence of the context points to an ellipsis in Paul's style in v. 5, "Such condensed and strictly speaking inaccurate expressions are common in language of a quasicolloquial kind."[16] Τῷ ὁμοιώματι (v. 5) is to be understood as an ethical dative with "a strong emphasis on the personal idea."[17] Paul's ellipsis may be fleshed out by adding τῷ Χριστῷ. The fuller clause would then read εἰ γὰρ σύμφυτοι γεγόναμεν τῷ Χριστῷ τῷ ὁμοιώματι τοῦ θανάτου αὐτοῦ, "For if we have been united with Christ in the likeness of his death."[18] This interpretation has the advantage of harmonizing with the overall theme of the context, union with Christ. It may be affirmed, therefore, that τῷ ὁμοιώματι does refer "to baptism itself" and "to the death of Christ itself."

An added comment—"The tenses of v. 5 also rule out the equation of ὁμοίωμα with baptism: the individual continues in the ὁμοίωμα (γεγόναμεν), and he certainly does not continue in the baptismal water!"[19]—is a bit of rhetoric that cannot be supported by exegesis.

A corollary to the foregoing discussion need detain us but briefly. On the assumption that baptism and resurrection are correlative ideas, Dunn finds it "a striking fact"[20] that they are not joined together in Rom. 6:4. As "a natural extension of the symbolism of baptism," the emergence of the convert from the waters of baptism would present a graphic representation of resurrection. Verse 4 is surprising "precisely because the balance of the sentence is disrupted by Paul's refusal to use this imagery."[21] This assertion raises some obvious questions. Is the balance of the sentence "disrupted?" Has Paul "refused" to use this imagery? Or, is the resurrection imagery represented by another figure of speech? The answers to these questions are found in Paul's use of the metaphor, "we too might walk in newness of life" (καινότητι ζωῆς). Seen in relation to the context, it is a synonymous parallelism with the resurrection motif, for through his spiritual rebirth, the Christian participates in the resurrection life of Christ here and now. The Christian's spiritual resurrection is the pledge of his future bodily resurrection. Since the convert rises from the baptismal waters to walk "in newness of life," it is apparent that Paul does combine the idea of baptism and resurrection in v. 4.

This interpretation is consistent with the grammatical structure of v. 4.[22] The comparison is between Christ's resurrection life and the convert's "newness of life" = resurrection life. In the comparison, Paul alters the second metaphor on stylistic grounds without changing the comparison between Christ's resurrection and the spiritual resurrection of the baptisand. This may be illustrated in the following paraphrase, "just as Christ was raised from the dead . . . so too we were raised from our baptism into his death, that we should henceforth walk in his resurrection life."

That baptism and resurrection were correlative ideas in the theology of Paul is made clear by the parallel passage in Col. 2:12, "you were buried with him in baptism in which also you were raised with him." The juxtaposition of baptism and resurrection in Col. 2:12 lends credibility to the contention that baptism and resurrection are correlatives in Rom. 6.

Paul's reference to the believer's future physical resurrection (v. 5) does not negate this interpretation. To argue that the tenses of v. 5 "rule out the equation of ὁμοίωμα with baptism" is hardly apropos. In Paul's thought, the resurrection of the Christian is both present and future. The future physical resurrection is simply the culmination of the resurrection life begun at conversion (Rom. 8:23). To identify the resurrection exclusively with the "future somatical resurrection"[23] would be to press text out of context, a context in which the Christian life is a present participation in the resurrection life of Jesus. It is a participation begun, in Paul's metaphorical language, when the believer rises from the baptismal waters to "walk in newness of life."

Rom. 2:28–29; 7:4–6

Rom. 2:28f. and 7:4–6 are lumped together because they are "closely related through the πνεῦμα/γράμμα [spirit/letter] antithesis."[24] What is not made clear, however, in the ensuing exposition is that the context of 2:28f., beginning at least with 2:12, is a discussion of the law (Torah). Both circumcision (v. 25 f.) and the spirit/letter antithesis (v. 29) are, therefore, to be interpreted in their relation to the law, as a passage in II Cor 3:7—"carved in letters of stone"—also suggests.

The teaching of Rom. 2:28f. is summarized by Dunn in stark polarities, "external rites are not to be identified or confused with internal realities; external rites are futile and invalid, even though given by God, unless there is a corresponding internal reality" (cf. v. 25).[25] Conversely, one may be prompted to ask, if the corresponding internal reality is present, are the external rites then effective and valid? The internal reality in v. 25 is obedience to the law/Torah; in v. 29 it is described metaphorically as circumcision of the heart.[26]

When the internal reality is described as obedience to the law/Torah, contextual exegesis requires that the spirit/letter antithesis be understood in relation to the theme of the law. Inasmuch as the common denominator of the context is the law/Torah, the antithesis in v. 28f. is between the Jew whose observance of the law is in the letter and the one whose obedience to the law is in the spirit. Therefore, to interpret πνεύματι as Holy Spirit (as Dunn does)[27] upsets the symmetry of the antithesis, that is, *letter* of the law versus *spirit* of the law. The essence of the antithesis is epitomized in the comment that "πνεῦμα *here* is not man's spirit, nor properly the Holy Spirit, but *the spirit* as opposed to *the letter* of the Jewish law."[28]

When the internal reality is described as circumcision of the heart (περιτομὴ καρδίας), an understanding of the metaphor is essential to the interpretation of the passage. The figure is rooted in the OT where a twofold usage is discernible. In Deut 10:16 circumcision of the heart is something the Israelite is called upon to do for himself, "Circumcise [περιτεμεῖσθε, LXX, *circumcise yourselves*] therefore the foreskin of your heart and be no longer stubborn." Since, in this sense, circumcision of the heart is something the individual was called upon to do for himself, Rom. 2:26 may, in this sense, refer to the Gentile who also keeps the precepts of Torah, even though uncircumcised, and thereby achieves for himself circumcision of the heart by his obedience to the law. Thus he achieves for himself the internal reality.

On the other hand, circumcision of the heart is something that God will do for a restored Israel, "And the Lord your God will circumcise your heart and the heart of your offspring, so that you will love the Lord your God with all your heart and with all your soul, that you may live" (Deut. 30:6). It is important for the application of this text to the present discussion to note that the context here is an eschatological one.

The antithesis in v. 28f. is between the Jew whose circumcision is "external and physical" and one whose circumcision is of the heart. The question is how did the latter arrive at his circumcision of the heart? Did he circumcise his own heart by obedience to the law (Deut. 10:16), or did God perform the circumcision for him (Deut. 30:6)?

At the heart of the discussion is the interpretation of ἐν πνεύματι, *in spirit*, v. 29, "He is a Jew who is one inwardly, and real circumcision is a matter of the heart, spiritual (ἐν πνεύματι), and not literal (οὐ γράμματι)." Is Dunn's solution—"As in II Cor. 3:6 the πνεῦμα/γράμμα antithesis must be understood as the Holy Spirit"[29]—the correct one? Grammatically and contextually, we have had reason to challenge this conclusion. However, the question remains unanswered.

How is this circumcision to be accomplished in the messianic age? Is it something Christians do for themselves (Deut. 10:16)? Is it something done for them by the Lord (Deut. 30:6)? Or is there a sense in which it is a divine-human synergism?[30]

In the NT, prophetic eschatology is fulfilled, as we have argued, in Jesus' first coming. The messianic age inaugurated by Him provides an eschatological context in which to pose the question: What then is the significance of circumcision in the messianic age? The context of Col. 2:11–13 contributes to an understanding of the subject. There circumcision is equated with baptism, e.g., "περιτομὴ ἀχειροποίητος Col. 2:11a = περ(ιτομῇ) τοῦ Χριστοῦ b, by which baptism is meant."[31] "A circumcision made without hands" = "the circumcision of Christ" equals *baptism*. This conclusion stands in unequivocal contradiction to the claim that "external rites and internal realities belong to distinct and even antithetical spheres, so that one cannot be said to be performed or effected by or through the other."[32] The antinomy between "external rites" and "internal realities as "antithetical spheres" reflects the anti-sacramental bias of the author more clearly than it does Paul's understanding of circumcision in the messianic age.

The equation, baptism = circumcision, is illustrated in the cultural milieu of "Hellenistic Jews [who] did not enforce circumcision in the case of proselytes affirming that baptism is sufficient." Thus "in the opinion of a very influential and important class of Jews, circumcision and baptism were analogous rites."[33]

That baptism is the real focus in Dunn's discussion of the spirit/letter antithesis becomes apparent in his assertion that "When we realize that Paul thinks of circumcision of the heart in terms of the Spirit, it is only a small step to parallel circumcision of the flesh and circumcision of the heart with baptism in water and baptism in the Spirit."[34] The extension of the spirit/letter antithesis to baptism in water and baptism in the Spirit is a category mistake, for (water) baptism is circumcision of the heart in the messianic age.

Even the expression "antithetical spheres" reveals more of the commentator's world-view than it does of Paul's, or the Scriptures at large for that matter. In the biblical world-view, Spirit and matter form a continuum, and it is this (open) continuum with its frank acknowledgment of the miraculous that is a scandal to an outmoded physics.

Jesus anointed blind eyes with clay made of His spittle, then sent the blind man to wash in the pool of Siloam, and he "came back seeing" (John 9:6f.). Jesus, in turn, sent out the Twelve, who "anointed with oil many that were sick and healed them'' (Mark 6:13; cf. James 5:14). The early disciples carried their sick into the streets of Jerusalem so that Peter's shadow might at least touch them, "and they were all healed" (Acts 5:15f.). In Ephesus handkerchiefs and aprons were carried from Paul's body to the sick, "and diseases left them" (Acts 19:11f.), while at Troas Paul's embrace restored Eutychus to life (Acts 20:10).

It is a world-view in which water is changed into wine (John 2:1ff.), bread and wine become the body and blood of our Lord (Matt. 26:26ff.; Mark 14:22ff.; Luke 22:17ff.; I Cor. 11:23ff.), and baptism is *"the bath of regeneration and renewal by the* the Holy Spirit.''[35]

A brief word is in order regarding Rom. 7:4–6 to round out this discussion. Since he says, "The thought is therefore no different from that of 6.2–6, and what I said there applies here,''[36] the reader is referred to our response to the same comments on Rom. 6:1–14.

Rom. 8:1–27

In the discussion of Rom. 8:1–27, the key verse for the conversion-initiation thesis is v. 9. Pentecostals would agree that "Anyone who does not have the Spirit of Christ does not belong to him." What the Pentecostal does insist upon is that the biblical pattern reflects a twofold action of the Holy Spirit, first in regeneration and second in the gift of the Spirit for power-in-mission. Both aspects of the Spirit's activity are present in Paul's thought. For instance, in the discussion of the context of Rom. 8:9 the polarities between "death" versus "life" and "in the flesh" versus "in the Spirit" stress the operation of the Holy Spirit in regeneration. On the other hand, Rom. 15:18, 19 are the epitome of Paul's evangelistic labors "by word and deed, in the power of signs and wonders, in the power of the Spirit." The Rom. 8:9 context is a theological commentary that interprets the Johannine view of the vivifying action of the Holy Spirit, while the context of Rom. 15:18, 19 affirms the Lukan theme of the gift of the Spirit for power-in-mission. The power of the Spirit, operative through Paul's words *and deeds,* resulted in "the obedience of the Gentiles."

In our judgment, the thesis of conversion-initiation does not supply an adequate rationale for reducing to one these disparate contexts. Lacking specific documentation to the contrary, the best that can be said for the conversion-initiation paradigm is that it is a speculative reconstruction. Paul's own experience of conversion and baptism in the Spirit (three days later) reflects a knowledge of the theological emphases of both John and Luke. It is perhaps more accurate to say that it reflects a knowledge of a common deposit of apostolic faith and experience. From the Pentecostal perspective, therefore, any attempt to find conversion-initiation contexts by the arbitrary harmonizing of John with Luke and with Paul must be rejected. Each must be allowed to speak for himself before a comprehensive theology of the Spirit can be constructed.

Nothing that has been adduced thus far, as evidence against this understanding of both the Scriptures and his experience, is sufficient to alter the Pentecostal's conviction regarding the integrity of this position.

Rom. 10:9–17

Only one response is called for in answer to the conversion-initiation arguments here. Once again, the forced exegesis of the conversion-initiation hypothesis serves to underline its inherent contradictions. It is claimed, for example, "that for Paul the act of faith is inseparable from the public confession of faith = the public act of committal = the public act of calling upon the Lord. *Until that act there is no saving faith.*"[37] Contrast this assertion with Paul's own experience. For Paul, "calling upon his name" is inseparable from his baptism (Acts 22:16). Yet before his baptism, he had received the Holy Spirit through the laying on of Ananias's hands. Are we to entertain seriously the notion that even though he had received the Holy Spirit, Paul did not have "saving faith" until he called upon the name of the Lord at his baptism?

Notes

[1]Dunn, op. cit., pp. 139–151.
[2]Ibid., p. 139.
[3]Bauer, Arndt, Gingrich.
[4]F. F. Bruce, *The Acts of the Apostles* (2nd ed.: Grand Rapids: Wm. B. Eerdmans Publishing Company, 1960), p. 95.
[5]Dunn, op. cit., p. 139.
[6]Ibid.
[7]Ibid., p. 140.
[8]Ibid.
[9]Ibid.
[10]Ibid., p. 145; italics added.
[11]Ibid.
[12]Ibid.
[13]Ibid.
[14]Ibid., pp. 142, 143.

[15]Ibid., p. 142; n. 11.

[16]William Sanday and Arthur C. Headlam, *A Critical and Exegetical Commentary on the Epistle to the Romans, The International Critical Commentary* (13th ed.; New York: Charles Scribner's Sons, 1911), p. 158.

[17]A. T. Robertson and W. Hersey Davis, *A New Short Grammar of the Greek New Testament* (New York: Harper & Brothers [c] 1933), p. 243.

[18]NASB et al. supply "with him."

[19]Dunn, op. cit., p. 143.

[20]Ibid.

[21]Ibid.

[22]ὥσπερ introduces "the protasis of a comparison, the apodosis of which begins w(ith) οὕτως (just) as . . . so," Bauer, Arndt, Gingrich.

[23]Dunn, op. cit., p. 143.

[24]Ibid., p. 146.

[25]Ibid.

[26]Cf. Deut. 10:16; 30:3; Jer. 4:4; 9:26; Ezek. 44:7; Acts 7:51.

[27]Dunn, op. cit., p. 146, n. 24.

[28]Henry Alford, *The Greek Testament,* II (Cambridge: Deighton, Bell, and Co., 1866), p. 368.

[29]Dunn, op. cit., p. 146.

[30]A comparison of the *middle voice* περιτεμεῖοθε, *circumcise yourselves* (Deut. 10:16, and the *middle voice* βάπτισαι, *get yourself baptized* (Acts 22:16), may suggest as much.

[31]Bauer, Arndt, Gingrich.

[32]Dunn, op. cit., p. 146.

[33]W. O. E. Oesterley, "Circumcision," *Dictionary of Christ and the Gospels,* ed. James Hastings, I (New York: Charles Scribner's Sons, 1917), pp. 330, 331.

[34]Dunn, op. cit., p. 146.

[35]Bauer, Arndt, Gingrich.

[36]Dunn, op. cit., p. 146.

[37]Dunn, op. cit., p. 151; italics added.

Chapter 12

The Later Epistles of Paul

Col. 1:13

Paul's prayer for the Colossians (1:9–13) is epitomized in his petition, "that you may be filled with the knowledge of his will in all spiritual (πνευματικῇ) wisdom and understanding" (v. 9). Verse 13 is a metaphorical allusion to the beginning of their Christian experience, e.g., "He [the Father] has delivered us from the dominion of darkness and transferred us to the kingdom of his beloved Son."

Dunn's exposition of this text is designed to support the conclusion that "This work of God (through the Spirit) takes place wholly on the spiritual plain—any relation it has to baptism is purely subsidiary to the thought here."[1] But the denigration of baptism is wholly gratuitous inasmuch as there is no reference at all to the role, or efficacy, of baptism in the text. The only apparent justification for its introduction here seems to be the author's debate with Käsemann, et al., over their respective theological presuppositions. Whether then μετέστησεν, "he has transferred," is a "conversion aorist" or a "baptismal aorist"[2] is not at issue in the text.

The gratuitous nature of the debate is reflected in an ad hominem comment with which the discussion begins:

> In turning to Colossians, Ephesians and the Pastorals we enter the most disputed part of the Pauline corpus. They include a number of passages which both Pentecostal and sacramentalist have sought to interpret to their own advantage.[3]

However, the indictment cuts both ways, for this is precisely what Dunn has done in interpreting "conversion-initiations contexts" to his own advantage.

As a general theological statement, one does not take exception to the following generalization. This does not apply to some questions of methodology, however.

> Paul throughout Colossians refrains from ascribing any salvific work to the Spirit . . . But that the Spirit is the agent of God's redemptive act in the spiritual transfer from the dimension of darkness to the kingdom of the Son is implied.[4]

119

The Pentecostal is aware of what is to him a curious oversight in the supporting argumentation. This is primarily an appeal to Paul's use in the context of expressions like "spiritual wisdom," "bearing fruit," "power," "glory," and "joy," while at the same time seeing nothing significant in the juxtaposition of bearing fruit and power.

We have already argued that bearing the fruits of the Holy Spirit (Gal. 5:22) is evidence of spiritual life, i.e., the new birth. On the other hand, "Believers are ἐν πάσῃ δ(υνάμει) δυναμούμενοι *equipped* w(ith) all power . . . esp(ecially) the apostles and other men of God . . . the *power* that works wonders."[5] The Pentecostal naturally sees in this the twofold action of the Holy Spirit in regeneration and enduement with power-in-mission. Furthermore, the phrase "in all spiritual wisdom and understanding" (ἐν πάσῃ σοφίᾳ καὶ συνέσει πνευματικῇ)reflects a kinship with "the word of wisdom," one of the supernatural charisms of the Spirit (I Cor. 12:1ff.).

Methodologically, there have been recurrent instances in which the rigidity of the conversion-initiation paradigm has imposed a forced and unnatural interpretation on the text. Dunn's exposition is no exception. In the effort to "spiritualize" the text, he asserts that "πνεῦμα in Eph. 1:17 is the Holy Spirit referred to in the same way as in Rom. 8:15."[6] By inference then the συνέσει πνευματικῇ, "spiritual understanding" (Col. 1:9), is to be understood in the same way. The assumption is debatable. In both Eph. 1:17 and Rom. 8:15 πνεῦμα, *spirit,* is lower case. For instance, in Eph. 1:17 Paul prayed that God would give to them "a new (human) spirit . . . 'of wisdom and revelation.'"[7] In Rom. 8:15 the "spirit of slavery" and "the spirit of adoption" are both lower case.

Col. 2:11–13

It is easier to demonstrate that baptism is a constituent part of Col. 2:11–13 than it is of the former text. In v. 11 the circumcision made without hands equals the circumcision of Christ, "by which baptism is meant."[8] The equation, circumcision = baptism, has solid support among the early church fathers. St. Hilary of Poitier (b. A.D. 300) commenting on Col. 2:11–12, speaks of the circumcision of Christ as burial with him in baptism.[9] John of Damascus (A.D. 676–754/780), whom Philip Schaff called "the greatest systematic theologian of the Eastern church,"[10] in commenting on the same passage speaks of holy baptism as circumcision from sin.[11]

Dunn, however, dissents saying, "Paul is not speaking here of baptism under the figure of circumcision; he is speaking directly of circumcision of the heart."[12] Once again the conclusion falters in the face of the exegesis of the passage. How, or when, does circumcision of the heart take place, if not in baptism? Verse 11 begins, "In him also you were circumcised" (περιετμήθητε), followed by two ἐν-phrases; ἐν τῇ ἀπεκδύσει, "in stripping off" (i.e., the fleshly body), and ἐν τῇ περιτομῇ, "in the circumcision" (i.e., of Christ). These two prepositional phrases modify (adverbially) the verb περιετμήθητε, "you were circumcised." That is to say, the fleshly body was stripped off in the circumcision of Christ, i.e., in baptism. One may note here the affinity of this view of baptism with Luke's in Acts 22:16.

Thus far we can agree, at least in principle, with the assessment that "The first two ἐν-phrases . . . stand very close together as one phrase dependent on περιετμήθητε."[13] The critical question, however, is the relationship of the next clause in the text, "you were buried with him in baptism" (συνταφέντες αὐτῷ ἐν τῷ βαπτίσματι *(sic)*, v. 12), to the verb περιετμήθητε (v. 11)? Dunn's response that "ἐν τῷ βαπτίσματι *(sic)* stands in a separate, though closely related clause, governed by συνταφέντες"[14] does not really address the syntax of the passage.

The expression "separate" must not be understood to mean *separated*. Syntactically, the emphasis is upon "closely related." The question then is how closely related is the clause governed by συνταφέντες to the verb περιετμήθητε? Συνταφέντες, "having been buried," is a circumstantial participle that introduces a hypotactic, subordinate clause. This subordinate clause stands in an adverbial relationship to the verb of the principal clause. The adverbial modifier (i.e., the circumstantial participle) may express time, manner, means, or some other circumstance affecting the antecedent verb. (Parenthetically, it should also be noted that the participle is followed by the associative instrumental αὐτῷ "with him"). What Paul is saying then to the Colossians is that they were circumcised with the circumcision of Christ by means of, or when they were buried with him in, baptism.

Verse 12 is another crux in the interpretation of the passage. As in circumcision it is flesh that is severed, so in baptism it is the severing, i.e., the "putting off" (ἀπεκδύσει) of "the body of flesh" that is the pregnant metaphor. The burial of "the body of flesh" in baptismal circumcision predicates a resurrection in conformity with the economy of redemption. The change of metaphor to resurrection (v. 12b) is not a change of subject; it is an extension of the metaphor of baptismal circumcision.

Whether then the ἐν ᾧ καὶ in v. 12b refers to Christ, *in whom also* (you were raised), or to baptism, *in which also* (you were raised), it does not alter the baptismal motif, as the following συν-compound verb, συνηγέρθητε, "you were raised with (him)" implies.

Contextually, we can find no support for the opinion that "Paul is not still thinking in terms of baptism; nor is he thinking of emergence from the baptismal waters as a resurrection or as symbolical of resurrection."[15] But this is precisely the intent of the passage. The tense of the verb "you were raised" (συνηγέρθητε) is aorist, as are all the verbs in vv. 11, 12. Although the aorists are punctiliar in action, they derive their time reference from the periphrastic perfect, ἐστε ἐν αὐτῷ πεπληρωμένοι, "in him you have been made full/complete," in v. 10.

In the context, the resurrection contemplated is a past event; it cannot refer to the future "somatical resurrection." Thus, their baptismal circumcision (v. 11), their burial with him in baptism (v. 12a), and their resurrection with (him) (v. 12b) are past events, the effects of which continue into the present.

The next question is a logical one. If they were buried with him in baptism, when were they raised with him? The one answer that makes sense in the context is that their baptismal union *with him* predicates union *with him* in his resurrection (Rom. 6). The recurrence of the circumcision metaphor in v. 13 points also to this conclusion, "You who were dead in trespasses and the uncircumcision of your flesh, God made alive together with him (αὐτῷ)." The passage echoes also the "newness of life" to which the baptisand is raised from his baptism.

Eph. 1:13–14; 4:30

The conversion-initiation argument here, based principally on Eph. 1:13f., is twofold. (1) Some Pentecostal writers are faulted for interpreting the aorist participle πιστεύσαντες, "*having* also believed,"[16] as action antecedent to the verb ἐσφραγίσθητε, "you were sealed." (2) It is categorically affirmed that "any identification of the seal of the Spirit with baptism or confirmation is to be rejected."[17]

The text reads in the KJV, "in whom also *after* that ye believed (πιστεύσαντες) ye were sealed with that Holy Spirit of promise."[18] The view of those Pentecostal exegetes who stress the antecedent action of the aorist participle is objected to as "a fundamental misunderstanding of Greek grammar,"[19] in spite of the immediately subjoined concession that "The aorist participle does in fact *usually* express antecedent action."[20] The contradiction posed by this concession is resolved (?) however, by an appeal to the context, "but it is the context, not the grammatical form which determines this."[21]

The argument is a non sequitur. While faulting Pentecostals for "a fundamental misunderstanding of Greek grammar," he does not resolve the differences in viewpoint by a "correct" understanding of grammar. In fact, he abandons the grammar altogether, and appeals to the context without resolving the grammatical issue raised by the Pentecostals. His indictment of Pentecostal exegesis lacks a bill of particulars and should, therefore, be regarded as wholly gratuitous.

Even the argument from the context itself lacks sufficient specificity to be evaluated. Once again, the issue is settled by a preconceived conversion-initiation schema. The aorist participle is here circumstantial, and time reference is a function of the circumstantial participle. In the face of the admission that the "aorist participle does in fact *usually* express antecedent action," we are not told how the context here alters its "usual" grammatical function. Obviously, the judgment in favor of coincident, rather than antecedent action, is an a priori of the conversion-initiation thesis. We are simply informed that "the context here indicates that we should take the two verbs as the two sides of the one event: it was when they believed that God sealed them with the Spirit."[22] In addition to this, and apart from the preconceptions of the conversion-initiation paradigm, it is not clear how the added appeal to Gal. 3:2 supports this conclusion.

We conclude then, on methodological grounds alone, that the Pentecostal is justified in calling attention to the circumstantial nature of the participle. The appeal to the context does not negate the grammatical argument. As a matter of fact, since antecedent action is its "usual" function, we contend that the grammatical argument tips the scales in favor of the Pentecostal interpretation.

It is time now to raise an antecedent question that has been obscured by the assumptions of the conversion-initiation hypothesis. Is the seal of the Spirit here to be identified with the initial action of the Holy Spirit in conversion (Dunn has already rejected "any identification of the seal of the Spirit with baptism or confirmation"[23]), or with the subsequent Spirit-baptism for power-in-mission? By reducing these two actions of the Holy Spirit to one, the conversion-initiation thesis does not even consider the question. However, from the Pentecostal point of view, the question is a substantive one.

Of the former, it may be observed that baptism as a seal is a common image in early Christian literature. If, therefore, the seal of the Spirit is identified with the initial action of the Spirit in conversion/regeneration, then the identification of the seal with baptism is a natural consequence. In fact, the seal of the Spirit in Eph. 1:13 is interpreted by some contemporary scholars "of those who enter the Christian fellowship as being sealed with or by the Holy Spirit."[24]

Whether the identification of the seal of the Spirit with baptism is accepted or rejected depends in large measure upon two prior assumptions: (1) the seal of the Spirit is identified with conversion/regeneration and (2) one's understanding of the sacramental nature of baptism.

On the other hand, the same scholars referred to above note in regards to II Cor. 1:22 that "here σφ(ραγισάμενος) obviously means more than just 'provide w(ith) a mark of identification'. Rather it = 'endue with power from heaven', as plainly in J(ohn) 6:27."[25] This raises the question of the identification of the seal of the Spirit with Spirit-baptism for power-in-mission.

If the seal of the Spirit is identified with the gift of the Spirit for power-in-mission, then the grammatical question posed by πιστεύσαντες in Eph. 1:13 is indeed a live issue. The case for Spirit-baptism for power-in-mission predicates antecedent action of the circumstantial participle. Their believing is antecedent to their sealing. The reference becomes then perhaps the clearest allusion to a Pentecostal baptism in the Spirit in Paul's epistles, and its analogue would be the "Ephesian Pentecost" in Acts 19:1ff.

It will, of course, be recognized that we also appeal to the larger context in favor of the grammatical argument, not, however, as a substitute for, but as an illustration of, the grammatical sense. We simply refer the reader to our previous discussion of the "Ephesian Pentecost." Suffice it to say here, that in their case, baptism preceded the laying on of hands for the reception of the Holy Spirit. From the Pentecostal standpoint, it may be argued then that the faith commitment expressed in baptism preceded the reception of the gift (seal) of the Spirit for power-in-mission. The seal of the Spirit is, therefore, "endue(ment) with power from heaven," which is another way of saying Spirit-baptism for power-in-mission.

Eph. 2:4–6

The identification of Eph. 2:4–6 with baptism is made "principally on the grounds of the undoubtedly close parallel between 2:5 and Col. 2:13."[26] The identification with baptism is rejected because "Col.

2:13 . . . completely changed the metaphor from that to which baptism was attached.''[27] For the rebuttal of this claim, the reader is referred to the previous discussion of Col. 2:13 in this chapter.

Dunn's next sentence is an example of the forced exegesis that the conversion-initiation paradigm imposes on the biblical text. He says, "There is nothing of burial here, and the death spoken of is a pre-Christian state, not part of the conversion event.''[28] The reader will, no doubt, observe that the statement begins with an argument from silence ("There is nothing of burial here") and really contributes nothing to the understanding of the text.

It is the second clause, however, that must be challenged. Of course, "the death spoken of is a pre-Christian state," and contrary to the assertion above, *is* "part of the conversion event." It is *from* a pre-Christian state of death that the believer is raised by his identification with Christ's death and resurrection.

The significance of the passage is encapsulated in the three verbs, συνεζωοποίησεν, συνήγειρεν, and συνεκάθισεν. All three are συν-compound verbs and make it clear that believers are "made alive," "raised," and "seated" *with Christ*. The parallels with baptism in Col. 2:13 and Rom 6:1ff., are quite clear.

The assertion that their pre-Christian state of death is "not part of the conversion event" is contradicted by the affirmation that "The ref(erence) is to people who were dead in their sins, but through union w(ith) Christ have been made alive [συνεζωοποίησεν] by God together with him.''[29]

Death, burial, and resurrection with Christ cannot be detached from the conversion event, nor can they be detached from Paul's understanding of baptism.

Eph. 4:1–6

It is difficult, for one with no commitment to the conversion-initiation paradigm, to see how Paul's discussion of the "seven great unities" of Eph. 4:1–6 relates to "the respective roles of the Spirit and baptism in Christian conversion-initiation.''[30] The suppositional nature of the exposition is revealed in the author's recourse to the phrases: "This passage *appears to indicate*" (161); "we *would* have expected" (161); "This *probably implies*" (161); "Thus we *might* well say" (162); none of which are empirically verifiable. As one *would* anticipate (!)—and one is not disappointed—the conjectural nature of the argumentation results in a purely hypothetical conclusion, "The fact that baptism is included in the list *implies* that baptism was regarded as the only legitimate way for faith to come to [initial] visible expression."[31]

It is a *fact* that baptism is mentioned in the text, all the rest is simply speculation.

These assumptions relating to baptism have been addressed in other places, and no further reply is called for here except to call attention to an apparent error of fact in the exposition. If βάπτισμα is the *result* of baptizing, while βαπτισμός is the *act*, the claim "that in the Pauline use βάπτισμα is the external act of water-baptism as such and nothing more"[32] is in fact an error.

Eph. 5:25–27

The exposition of Eph. 5:25–27 involves a series of deductions from the context. (1) The bridal bath analogy is central. (2) The metaphor of husband and wife describes the relationship of Christ to the Church. (3) The *parousia* is a wedding wherein Christ presents (παραστήσῃ) the Church to himself as a bride. The "washing of water with the word" (τῷ λουτρῷ τοῦ ὕδατος) is interpreted as "the bridal bath which precedes and prepares for the wedding."[33]

In the wedding/parousia analogy, does the bridal bath refer to baptism or "to the inner cleansing and sanctifying operation of the Spirit?"[34] If the "washing of water with the word" is not baptism, what evidence is there for an eschatological "washing" preceding the eschatological "wedding?"

It is again the recurrent question of an assumed dichotomy between Spirit and baptism. The spots and wrinkles are, of course, a reference to sin, its taint and its consequences, and "As the bridal bath washes away all dirt and spots, so God's cleansing washes away all sin."[35] But this in itself is not sufficient to exclude baptism from participation in the spiritual cleansing. One is reminded again of the precedent in Acts 22:16 that identifies baptism with cleansing from sin, "Rise, and be baptized, and wash away your sins, calling on his name." That a dichotomy exists in the mind of the antisacramentalist is evident, but that a metaphysical dichotomy between Spirit and baptism existed in Paul's mind has not been demonstrated. As a matter of fact, in the history of doctrine such a metaphysical dichotomy has more to do with Plato than with Paul.

Neither is it clear that Paul uses *water* in a metaphorical sense, as is implied in the generalization that Christ's "instrument of cleansing is not water but that which water so often signifies in Scripture—the Spirit."[36] The point at issue is not whether Scripture in the broad sense uses water metaphorically for Spirit, it does. The question is simply, does Paul use water in a metaphorical sense for Spirit? Several things need to be observed in this connection. First, the text explicitly says "water." It does not mention the Spirit. Second, this is the *only* text in the acknowledged Pauline corpus that uses ὕδωρ, "water." There is, therefore, no direct evidence from which to establish a precedent for attributing to Paul a metaphorical sense to "the washing of water with the word." Third, all the metaphorical uses of ὕδωρ are found in the Johannine literature.[37]

A further objection to the understanding that the "washing of water" alludes to baptism simply trivializes the discussion, viz., "To say that the Church is literally washed in water is rather artificial."[38] The whole is the sum of its parts. To push the metaphor of the bridal bath to mean the Church collectively, is to contradict the admission that "It is in and by the Spirit's incorporation into the Body, the Church, that one participates in the Spirit's cleansing and sanctifying of the Church."[39] If then one participates (individually) in the Spirit's cleansing when one is incorporated into the Church, the "washing of water with the word" is also an individual, and not a collective, experience of the "bridal bath." The aorist participle "having cleansed" (καθαρίσας) refers contextually to a past event, that is, to baptism, and not to an eschatological bath before the parousia.

It is, furthermore, a moot point indeed to claim that "The verb which describes the cleansing (καθαρίζειν) has long since left the cultic sphere of ritual purity, and in NT religion it stands for a spiritual and moral cleansing and purifying."[40] That this claim is something less than certain is reflected in the following opinion, "Hb 9:22f occupies an intermediate position [i.e., between the Levitical and the moral] since ceremon(ial) purification and moral purification merge, and the former becomes the shadow-image of the latter."[41] The additional claim that "ἁγιάζειν can only be referred to a spiritual operation"[42] does not dissolve τῷ λουτρῷ τοῦ ὕδατος into a metaphor of ἁγιάζειν. The circumstantial participle καθαρίσας, "having cleansed," argues against this, for it describes *how* the Church/bride's sanctification is accomplished, namely, "by the washing of water with the word" = baptism.

What is rejected here is the conclusion that "Paul uses baptism primarily as a metaphor and a symbol."[43] If the bridal bath is itself the metaphor, baptism is its visible, tangible homologue.

Titus 3:5–7

Verses 4 and 5 are a crux in the interpretation of Titus 3:5–7, i.e., "he saved us (ἔσωσεν) . . . by the *washing* of regeneration (διὰ λουτροῦ παλιγγενεσίας) and *renewing* by the Holy Spirit (ἀνακαινώσεως πνεύματος ἀγίου), whom he poured out (ἐξέχεεν) upon us richly through Jesus Christ our Saviour."[44]

The suggestion favoring the Pentecostal thesis that λουτροῦ παλιγγενεσίας and ἀνακαινώσεως πνεύματος ἀγίου are *not* strictly synonymous, that they may indeed refer to distinctive events in the economy of redemption, has been dismissed too peremptorily by Dunn.[45] The following discussion will defend the view that "the washing of regeneration" equals conversion/regeneration, while the "renewing by the Holy Spirit" equals the ongoing work of the Holy Spirit subsequent to the initial conversion experience. One can see immediately a congruence with the Pentecostal view, however, that the latter refers to Pentecost is itself a moot point, The theme of "renewing by the Holy Spirit" fits better with the theme of maturation of the spiritual life. This is not, however, the focus of this response. At issue is the claim that the "washing of regeneration" and the "renewing by the Holy Spirit" are reduced to "the Pentecostal outpouring of the Spirit—the baptism in the Spirit—which effects the regeneration and renewal of salvation."[46] This assumption is categorically rejected.

The former is a single conversion/regeneration event, while the latter bespeaks the ongoing work of the Holy Spirit subsequent to the initial conversion experience. For instance, the cognate verb, ἀνακαινόω, is used in II Cor. 4:16 in precisely this way, "though our outer man is decaying, yet our inner man is being renewed (ἀνακαινοῦται) *day by day*."[47] Analogically, this would support a distinction between παλιγγενεσίας and ἀνακαινώσεως in Titus 3:5. As noted above, the former would refer to regeneration, the latter to the subsequent and ongoing spiritual renewal provided by the Holy Spirit. This view is trenchantly summarized thus, "Birth, natural or spiritual, must be a definite fact taking place at a particular moment; whereas renewing is necessarily a subsequent process, constantly operating."[48]

Even if one were to acquiesce momentarily to the view that

παλιγγενεσίας and ἀνακαινώσεως are synonomous, it cannot be proven thereby that Pentecost is "the regeneration and renewal of salvation." It is important for the exegesis of the passage to note that though the preposition (διά) is used only once, it is implied in both phrases, contrary to Dunn's view that "both phrases, λουτ. παλ. and ἀνακ. πν. ἀγ., are governed by the one διά."[49] Syntactically, "The genitive ἀνακαινώσεως depends on διά (which is actually inserted in the Harclean Syriac."[50] This reading is reflected in the RSV margin, "and through *renewing*." A second variant places διά before πνεύματος ἁγίου and is reflected in the NASB reading, "and renewing by the Holy Spirit."

These variant readings make explicit what is implicit in the Greek syntax. The assumption that "If the ideas had been distinct and the events involved separate, it would have been natural to repeat the διά"[51] imposes an arbitrary canon of style not dictated by the syntax and excluded in the variant readings above. One must, consequently, disagree with the dictum that "The NEB margin is therefore to be preferred: 'the water of rebirth and renewal by . . . ', with both παλ. and ἀνακ. being taken as dependent on λουτροῦ."[52] The net effect of making παλιγγενεσίας and ἀνακαινώσεως both dependent upon λουτροῦ is to confuse the metaphors, "the washing of regeneration and (washing) of renewal" *daily* (?).

The single use of the preposition may be explained syntactically as an ellipsis, and the passage makes better sense when read that way. On this understanding, the two prepositional phrases modify the verb ἔσωσεν. How? "By the washing of regeneration" and "by renewing of the Holy Spirit," or alternatively, "renewing by the Holy Spirit." Ἔσωσεν refers to a crisis (regeneration) that issues in a process (spiritual renewal) by the Holy Spirit in the economy of redemption.

The word ἀνακαίνωσις is uniquely Pauline. In addition to Titus 3:5, the noun is used in Rom. 12:2 of "the renewing of the mind." The cognate verb refers in II Cor. 4:6 to the renewing of our inner nature ἡμέρα καὶ ἡμέρα, "every day" and in Col. 3:10 to "being renewed in knowledge." In none of these instances is there a precedent for equating ἀνακαίνωσις in Titus 3:5 with the single event of regeneration.

Whether or not the following clause in v. 6, "whom he poured out (οὗ ἐξέχεεν) upon us *richly*,"[53] is an allusion to Pentecost is debatable. The only support for the assumption is the verbal correspondence with

Acts 2:17, 18, 33. The clause introduced by the relative pronoun οὗ is an epexegetical comment referring to the preceding πνεύματος ἁγίου by attraction. The Holy Spirit who renews us has been poured out richly upon us. The clause describes the measure in which God has poured out His Spirit, i.e., πλουσίως, *richly*, but not the occasion *when*.

To sum up then, reducing λουτροῦ παλιγγενεσίας and ἀνακαινώσεως πνεύματος ἁγίου to "the Pentecostal outpouring of the Spirit—the baptism of the Spirit—which effects the regeneration and renewal of salvation"—is to theologize a conclusion without adequate exegetical support from the context. It is decidedly inappropriate then to say, as Dunn does, that it constitutes a "decisive check to Pentecostal ideas both of conversion and Spirit-baptism."[54] Pentecostals have been around too long to be dismissed so lightly. Cyprian, bishop of Carthage (A.D. 200–258), voices a comment on Titus 3:5 that has a remarkably Pentecostal ring to it, "one is not born by the imposition of hands when he receives the Holy Ghost, but in baptism, so that being already born, he may receive the Holy Spirit."[55]

What then is the λουτροῦ παλιγγενεσίας? Most commentators accept baptism as the primary reference, and the exegesis of the text provides no reason to take issue with this. Even though the view is rejected that "παλιγγενεσίας and ἀνακαινώσεως are both dependent on λουτροῦ," one can agree that "neither can be independent of or separated from the Spirit,"[56] so long as the twofold action of the Spirit is kept in mind. The apostolic tradition linking water and Spirit ("unless one is born of water and the Spirit," John 3:5, and "the newness of life" identified with baptism, Rom. 6:40) cannot be ignored. Scripture does not polarize baptism and Spirit as symbol and reality into antithetical spheres. Nor does it, on the other hand, claim an efficacy for baptism *opera ex operato*.

Notes

[1]Dunn, op. cit., p. 152.
[2]Ibid., pp. 152, 153.
[3]Ibid., p. 152.
[4]Ibid.
[5]Bauer, Arndt, Gingrich.
[6]Dunn, op. cit., p. 152.
[7]Markus Barth, *Ephesians*, Vol. 34, *The Anchor Bible* (Garden City: Doubleday & Company, Inc., 1974), p. 148.
[8]Bauer, Arndt, Gingrich.

[9]*De Trinitate*, IX, 9.

[10]*History of the Christian Church*, IV (New York: Charles Scribner's Sons, 1886), p. 405.

[11]*De Fide Orthodoxa*, XXV.

[12]Dunn, op. cit., p. 153.

[13]Ibid.

[14]Ibid.

[15]Ibid., p. 154.

[16]NASB, italics added.

[17]Dunn, op. cit., p. 160.

[18]Italics added.

[19]Ibid., p. 159.

[20]Ibid., italics added.

[21]Ibid.

[22]Ibid.

[23]Ibid., p. 160.

[24]Bauer, Arndt, Gingrich.

[25]Ibid.

[26]Dunn, op. cit., p. 160.

[27]Ibid.

[28]Ibid.

[29]Bauer, Arndt, Gingrich.

[30]Dunn, op. cit., p. 162.

[31]Ibid., italics added.

[32]Ibid., p. 162. Cf. Hermann Cremer, *Biblical Theological Lexicon of New Testament Greek*, trans. by D. W. Simon and William Urwick (Edinburgh: T & T Clark, 1872), p. 105. A. T. Robertson, *Word Pictures in the New Testament*, IV (New York: Harper & Brothers Publishers, 1931), p. 535.

[33]Dunn, op. cit., p. 163.

[34]Ibid.

[35]Ibid.

[36]Ibid.

[37]W. F. Moulton and A. S. Geden, *A Concordance to the Greek Testament* (4th ed.; Edinburgh: T. & T. Clark, 1967).

[38]Dunn, op. cit., p. 163.

[39]Ibid., pp. 163, 164.

[40]Ibid., p. 164.

[41]Bauer, Arndt, Gingrich.

[42]Dunn, op. cit., p. 164.

[43]Ibid., p. 165.

[44]NASB, italics added.

[45]Dunn, op. cit., p. 166.

[46]Ibid., p. 166.

[47]NASB, italics added.

[48]Newport J. D. White, "The Epistle to Titus," Vol. IV, *The Expositors' Greek Testament* (Grand Rapids: Wm. B. Eerdmans Publishing Co., [n. d.]), p. 199.

[49]Dunn, op. cit., p. 166.

[50]White, loc. cit.

[51]Dunn, op. cit., p. 166.

[52]Ibid.

[53]NASB, italics added.

[54]Dunn, op. cit., p. 166.

[55]*The Epistles of Cyprian*, Vol. V, *The Ante-Nicene Fathers*, eds., Alexander Roberts and James Donaldson, trans. Ernest Wallis (American edition; Grand Rapids: Wm. B. Eerdmans Publishing Co., 1971) LXXIII.

[56]Dunn, op. cit., p. 168.

Chapter 13

The Johannine Pentecost?

In the discussion of "The Johannine Pentecost?"[1] an important concession is made to the Pentecostal position:

Our conclusion so far is simply that the Pentecostal thesis at this point cannot be entirely rejected: John may well have considered that the baptism in the Spirit was a second and distinct work of the Spirit in the spiritual experience of the first disciples.[2]

The crucial text is John 20:22, "he [Jesus] breathed on them, and said to them, 'Receive the Holy Spirit.'" A convergence with the Pentecostal exegesis is to be noted in the statement that in "John's use of ἐνεφύσησεν . . . John presents the act of Jesus as a new creation."[3] Dunn acknowledges the parallel with ἐνεφύσησεν . . . πνοὴν in Gen. 2:7 (LXX) and adds "Jesus is the author of the new creation as He was of the old (1.3)."[4] The reader must now be aware that this exposes a contradiction in the conversion-initiation thesis.

If "the Church properly conceived did not come into existence until Pentecost,"[5] this simply affirms the cliché that Pentecost is the birthday of the Church. On the other hand, if the insufflation of the Holy Spirit on the resurrection day (20:22) is a new creation (a "new birth"), did the apostolic community experience the new creation/regeneration twice, once on the resurrection day (20:22) and again at Pentecost? Not, of course, if John 20:22 is understood as a "Johannine Pentecost." If, however, John knew of two bestowals of the Spirit on the apostolic community, *both* of which were by definition regeneration, then this compounds the contradiction in the conversion-initiation paradigm. How can it be claimed that the "Church . . . did not come into existence until Pentecost," if the resurrection day is the day of the new creation?

Did John then "know of two bestowals of the Spirit, though recording only one?"[6] The Paraclete sayings may provide a key to the riddle.

John 14:16, 17: The First Paraclete Saying

In response to the prayer of Jesus, the Father will give (δώσει) another Paraclete, the Spirit of truth of whom it is said, "you know him (γινώσκετε), for he lives with you (μένει), and will be in you (ἔσται)."[7] The first two verbs, γινώσκετε and μένει, are present tense, and it misses the point to say, "Jesus' words [all three verbs] could not be true of the disciples until after the sending of the Spirit."[8] The ἄλλον παράκλητον, "another Paraclete" (v. 16), "has the obvious implication that Jesus has been a Paraclete."[9] It is to himself as the Paraclete that Jesus refers in the words, "he lives with you." For the third verb, whether one opts for the present ἔστιν or the future ἔσται, *he is/will be* (in you), the sense is essentially the same. The "other Paraclete" is given to fill the place of the Paraclete who must shortly return to the Father.

In John 14:16, 17 the Spirit is not *sent*, He is *given*, and the significance suggested by this distinction will become apparent as the exposition proceeds. In the three subsequent Paraclete texts, the Spirit will be sent (πέμψει). The verb δίδωμι, "I give," in relation to the action of the Spirit is associated with regeneration in John. In 4:14 the water that Jesus gives (δώσω) "will become in him a spring of water welling up to eternal life." The "rivers of living water" (7:39) are an obvious parallel to this. Once again in the bread of life discourse, it is the Father who gives (δίδωσιν) "the true bread from heaven" that "gives life to the world" (6:32, 33). It may be said of the Paraclete sayings, at least tentatively at this point, that the Spirit in His regenerating activity is given, not sent. It is important to note also that regeneration is an ontological bestowal of the Spirit and thereby parallels His creative action on the resurrection day (20:22). The context of the first Paraclete saying also supports the identification with 20:22. The ἔτι μικρόν, "yet a little while" (14:19), was understood by the Eastern Fathers generally as a "reference to the post-resurrection appearances of Jesus."[10] The cryptic, "I will manifest myself to him" (v. 21), also points to an understanding of the passage as post-resurrectional. Thus, the post-resurrectional context and the ontological bestowal of the Spirit in the first Paraclete saying combine to point to the Paschal impartation of the Spirit in 20:22.

There is, however, a marked difference in the remaining Paraclete sayings. These stress the functional, rather than the ontological aspect of the Spirit's being sent, a suggestion parallel with the Lukan texts in Acts.

John 14:26: The Second Paraclete Saying

The Father will send (πέμψει) the Holy Spirit in the Son's name, "and he will teach you all things." This function of the Spirit occurs after Pentecost, when the believers "devoted themselves to the apostles' teaching" (τῇ διδαχῇ, "teaching," "instruction," Acts 2:42).

John 15:26: The Third Paraclete Saying

Jesus himself will send (πέμψω) the Paraclete, the Spirit of truth "who proceeds from the Father." The Spirit of truth then "will bear witness" to Jesus, a statement made to the disciples regarding witnessing after their Spirit-baptism in Acts 1:8.

John 16:7ff.: The Fourth Paraclete Saying

In the final saying, Jesus will go away that He may send (πέμψω) the Paraclete, who when He is come "will convict the world of sin." As Peter addressed the assembled multitude on the day of Pentecost, the Spirit convicted them of sin—"they were cut to the heart" (Acts 2:37)—and prompted Peter's summons to "repent."

A close parallel also exists between the last three Paraclete sayings and Acts 2:33, viz., "and having received from the Father the promise of the Holy Spirit, he [Jesus] has poured forth this which you see and hear."

It is now possible to answer the question that prompted this discussion of the Paraclete sayings, namely, Did John know of two bestowals of the Spirit though recording only one? The evidence indicates that he did. The chronological sequence of events in John 20, the post-resurrectional context, and the ontological bestowal of the Spirit, recorded in the first Paraclete saying, (vis-à-vis the functional nature of the Spirit's being sent in the last three sayings) combine to support this conclusion. Thus from the Pentecostal perspective, it would require considerable ingenuity to make the last three Paraclete sayings, along with John 20:22, to refer to one Pentecostal outpouring of the Spirit. My friend David du Plessis aptly remarks, "The upper room on the resurrection day was a maternity ward, Pentecost was a baptismal service." But the so-called 'Johannine Pentecost' is not at issue in the debate inasmuch as we agree with Dunn that John 20:22, "substantiates the Pentecostals' principal claim—that the apostles were regenerate before Pentecost."[11]

Whether Jesus, or the believer, is the source of the rivers of living water (7:37) is debatable.[12] Whether or not John 7:37f. is to be connected with John 20:22 because of its relation to the Spirit's life-giving work[13] is more germane to the present discussion. The bone of contention here is the observation that the cryptic οὔπω γὰρ ἦν πνεῦμα "for that the Spirit was not yet," "is not to be interpreted ontologically but functionally. So far as the disciples' experience of the Spirit was concerned, until 20:22, the Spirit was not yet."[14] If, however, John 7:37— 39 is to be interpreted in the light of 20:22, then οὔπω γὰρ ἦν πνεῦμα must be understood ontologically. After all, we have been informed that the Paschal insufflation of the Spirit is a new creation. By way of contrast, the Pentecostal effusion of the Holy Spirit is to be interpreted functionally (Acts 1:8) and not ontologically. This functional nature of the Pentecostal outpouring of the Spirit is distinguished by the charismatic manifestations that accompanied it, for example, "this which you both see and hear" (Acts 2:33). Failure to distinguish these two actions of the Spirit in the experience of the apostles' underscores what must be regarded as a fundamental contradiction in the conversion-initiation hypothesis.

A review of the arguments for and against a Johannine Pentecost focuses upon a fundamental question. Does John impose a theological scheme at the expense of the chronological sequence of events? Dunn's conclusion runs counter to the hypothesis of a Johannine Pentecost. He says, "The chronological separateness of the various events recorded in 20 (including the time lapse between the death and resurrection of Jesus) is retained (20.1, 19, 26)."[15] This conclusion is undergirded by the observation that "the οὔπω (20.17) preserves a clear enough time-lapse between resurrection and ascension."[16]

Though "torn between the two interpretations," Dunn concedes that "the Pentecostal thesis at this point cannot entirely be rejected: John may well have considered that the baptism in the Spirit was a second and distinct work of the Spirit in the spiritual experience of the first disciples."[17]

This concession is not, however, to be understood as a capitulation to the Pentecostal hermeneutic. The debate focuses on one point, and one point only. The fulcrum upon which the conversion-initiation thesis rests is the assertion that "the chronological sequence of events in the lives of the apostles is unique and unrepeatable."[18] In other words, the experience of the apostles cannot be normative for later Christians. The point is apparently not negotiable, for is is affirmed without qualification that "it is with this further step that he [i.e., the Pentecostal] definitely misses the way."[19]

The argument in support of the claim that the apostolic experience was "unique and unrepeatable" rests upon a theological reconstruction of salvation history. It posits a "transition period between the dispensations . . . at least from Jesus' death to Pentecost, if not from the beginning of his ministry to Pentecost, if not from his birth to Pentecost."[20] To this argument we reply that the dispensational argument is simply special pleading.

To postulate a transition period in salvation history between the resurrection and Pentecost is to consign the apostolic community to a dispensational limbo. What has happened to the unity of the body? If one were to entertain seriously the notion that "the Church properly conceived did not come into existence until Pentecost,"[21] then between Passover and Pentecost the disciples belonged neither to the old covenant (that ended with the death of Jesus) nor to the new covenant (that on this assumption had not yet begun).

What is overlooked here is that the four Gospels, up to the death of Jesus, belong to the older economy. There is continuity in Torah, temple, sacrifice, and covenant until the Paschal announcement of Jesus of the new covenant in His blood. If one is looking for a transitional period, the words of institution at the Last Supper have a prior claim on our attention. Indeed, from the standpoint of a sacramental realism, it may be argued that with the words, "This cup is the new covenant in my blood" (I Cor. 11:25), the apostles entered proleptically into the new covenant.

The incarnation marked "the time fulfilled" (i.e., prophetic time) and "the (messianic) kingdom of God at hand" (Mark 1:15). The rejection and crucifixion of Jesus radically altered the course of salvation history. With it, "the kingdom of God at hand" became "the kingdom not yet." Prophetic "fulfillment" was changed into apocalyptic anticipation.[22] The incarnation, life, ministry, and crucifixion belong to the older economy of salvation history. The resurrection, Pentecost, and the parousia, all belong equally to the new age.

The death of Jesus ended "in one fell stroke" the old covenant. The crucifixion was not a transitional period, it was the decisive event that terminated the old order. The Mosaic covenant was sealed with the sacrificial blood of animals. The new covenant was sealed with the sacrificial blood of the Lamb of God. With the Paschal impartation of the Holy Spirit, the disciples of Jesus entered into the resurrection life of Jesus. That moment marked the birth of the Church, for their new birth and the birth of the Church are one and the same.

To concede, on the one hand, that the apostles were regenerated by the Paschal bestowal of the Spirit, and to contend, on the other hand, that the Church did not come into existence until Pentecost, is a contradiction in terms. If the Church was not "born" until Pentecost, into what then were the apostles "born again" on the resurrection day?

To persist in this contradiction is simply to compound confusion, for if the apostles "were regenerate before Pentecost"[23] (i.e., fifty days before), yet Pentecost marks the receiving of "the Spirit in his cleansing, regenerating, baptismal power,"[24] we ask again an obvious question. Were the apostles regenerated twice? After all they did receive both the Paschal insufflation and the Pentecostal baptism in the Spirit. The obvious contradiction places the argument in the category of special pleading. As a matter of fact, the way in which the argument is stated confirms the charge of special pleading:

John certainly shows that it may not be possible to equate Spirit-baptism with regeneration, *but only in the case of the apostles*. His theological message at this point indicates (and Luke and Paul certainly show) that from Pentecost onward he who believes receives the Spirit in his cleansing, regenerating, baptismal power, bringing the forgiveness and life of the new dispensation.[25]

To speak of regeneration in the context of the Pentecostal baptism in the Spirit is to put words in Luke's mouth. The Greek equivalent, παλιγγενεσία, is found only in Matt. 19:28, in an eschatological context, and in Titus 3:5, in the sense of personal rebirth. The action of the Holy Spirit in terms of a personal rebirth is not a Lukan theme. Even the favorite Johannine word associated with the new birth, γεννάω, is not found in this sense in Luke, just as John does not use the Lukan δύναμις to describe the Spirit's activity.

It is of the utmost importance to note that Dunn's solution is a theological construct. But theology cannot be at variance with exegesis, and from the Pentecostal point of view, theology and exegesis have parted company here in the conversion-initiation thesis. Even Acts 2:38, appealed to frequently as the incontrovertible text in support of the conversion-initiation scheme, does not support this interpretation, for the context of "the gift of the Holy Spirit"[26] refers to the Pentecostal baptism for power-in-mission. Hermeneutical integrity requires that it be interpreted in the light of its context, and at no point in the account of Pentecost does Luke refer to the gift of the Holy Spirit as "receiv (ing) the Spirit in his cleansing, regenerating, baptismal power, bringing the forgiveness and life of the new dispensation." What Luke does speak of specifically is a "baptism in" (Acts 1:5), "filling with" (Acts

2:4) the Holy Spirit for power-in-mission (Acts 1:8)—that and nothing more.

From the Pentecostal perspective on Scripture, the following assumption is irreconcilable with the text of Scripture itself. Reference is made here to the categorical statement that

> The Baptism in the Spirit, as always, is primarily initiatory, and only secondarily an empowering. The fact is that the phrase "baptism in the Spirit" is *never* directly associated with the promise of power, but is always associated with entry into the messianic age or the Body of Christ.[27]

One might well ask how the claim that "the phrase 'baptism in the Spirit' is *never* directly associated with the promise of power" is to be reconciled with Luke 24:49, "And behold, I am sending forth the promise of My Father upon you; but stay in the city until you are *clothed with power* from on high."[28] The sequel in Acts 1:4 makes it clear that "the promise of the Father" is the Pentecostal baptism in the Spirit (Acts 1:5) for power-in-mission (Acts 1:8). By way of contrast, there is no hint in these contexts of initiation into either the messianic age or the Body of Christ. The *only* reason Luke assigns here for their waiting to receive "the promise of the Father" is power. It is the same theme of power in witnessing repeated in the narrative of Acts and epitomized in an autobiographical reminiscence of Paul in Rom. 15:19, "by the power of signs and wonders, by the power of the Holy Spirit."

The discussion of the "Johannine Pentecost" has served to confirm the view that the new birth by the Spirit cannot be identified with the baptism in the Spirit for power. The critique of the conversion-initiation thesis has also shown that the sequence, the new birth followed by a subsequent baptism in the Spirit for power-in-mission, is not to be confined to the experience of the apostles alone. It is, in fact, a counsel of confusion to attempt to confine it to a dispensational transitional period in the experience of the apostles. It is clearly the normative pattern of Christian spirituality throughout the period covered by the book of Acts. Nor does it end with the termination of the apostolic age.

In the fourth century, a twofold sequence in the Spirit's activity is noted by St. John Chrysostom (A.D. 347–407). He identified the Johannine impartation of the Spirit with the power to remit sins and the Pentecostal baptism in the Spirit with the power to work miracles.[29] The distinction is a provocative one. The distinction, according to this paradigm, is between ἐξουσία (ontological) and δύναμις (functional) power. Jesus' power (ἐξουσία) to forgive sins (Mark 2:10) derives from who He is incarnationally (i.e., the Son of God). His power (δύναμις) to work miracles derives from His Spirit-baptism (Luke 4:14, 18f.). The apostles' power (ἐξουσία) to remit sins derives from who they are by virtue of a new creation (i.e., sons of God; John 1:12; 20:22). Their power (δύναμις) to work miracles derives from their baptism in the Spirit (Acts 1:8).

If the experience of the apostles was normative for Christian experience in the infancy of the Church, then it is normative for Christian experience today. Peter said as much in his sermon on the day of Pentecost, "the promise [of the Father = the baptism in the Holy Spirit for power-in-mission] is to you and to your children [your descendants] and to all that are far off [the Gentiles], every one whom the Lord our God calls to him" (Acts 2:39).

If God is still calling "all who are far off," and he is, then the promise is still in effect, and the apostolic experience is normative for Christian experience today. The apostles are not separated from us by a dispensational divide. Their experience is our inheritance today.

Notes

[1]Dunn, op. cit., pp. 173–182.
[2]Ibid., p. 178.
[3]Ibid., p. 180.
[4]Ibid.
[5]Ibid., p. 51.
[6]Ibid., p. 177.
[7]NIV.
[8]Dunn, op. cit., p. 182.
[9]Raymond E. Brown, *The Gospel According to John*, Vol. 29A, *The Anchor Bible* (Garden City: Doubleday & Company, Inc., [1970]), p. 644.
[10]Brown, op. cit., p. 645.
[11]Dunn, op. cit., p. 181.
[12]For a survey of the literature on the variant punctuations of the text, cf. Dunn, op. cit., p. 179f., and Brown, op. cit., p. 319f.
[13]Dunn, op. cit., p. 180. Cf. also 4:14.
[14]Ibid.
[15]Ibid., p. 176.
[16]Ibid.
[17]Ibid., p. 178.
[18]Ibid.
[19]Ibid.
[20]Ibid., p. 181.
[21]Ibid., p. 51.

[22]Cf. Matt. 24:1ff.; Mark 13:1ff.; Luke 21:5ff.
[23]Dunn, op. cit., p. 181.
[24]Ibid., p. 182.
[25]Ibid.
[26]Cf. Acts 10:45; 11:17.
[27]Dunn, op. cit., p. 54; italics added.
[28]NASB, italics added.
[29]*Homilies on the Gospel of St. John*, LXXXVI.

Chapter 14

John 3:5

The chapter, "The Spirit and Baptism in John's Gospel,"[1] undertakes to answer the question, "Does John give us to understand that the Spirit is mediated through the sacrament of baptism?"[2] From the opening question to the final conclusion, the argumentation is a case study in methodology. The argument proceeds from assumption to supposition, from hypothesis to probability, from conjecture to conclusion in the following manner:

6.32, 35 and 45 *may also be* significant (184);
It is *just possible* (185);
we *might have inferred* from John's *silence* (185);
the Evangelist *seems to be* envisaging (186);
Is ch. 5 *perhaps* . . . a warning (187);
and *quite probably* Heb. 6.4 (187);
the *implication* is (187);
John *seems to* have taken over (187);
John *may have been* thinking (187);
There is *probably* a further imagery in mind (187);
John *probably intends* no symbolism (189);
he *does not mention* it (189);
This greatly lessens *the probability* (189);
It is *more likely* therefore (189);
it *would suggest* (189);
John *seems to be* . . . which he *assumes* (190);
The *most likely answer* is that the author *intended* (190);
If this is so, the reader *would then understand* (190);
This *seems to be* confirmed (191);
It is *more likely* (191);
had John *intended* . . . he *could hardly* have failed (191);
This *implies* either that . . . or (192);
The latter is *perhaps* the *more likely* view (192);
John's baptism *seems to have been* (192);
It *may be* that John is (193);
he *would surely* have mentioned it again (193);
the fact that he does not . . . *implies* (193);
he seeks to counter *by his silence* (194);
If Brown is right in his *conjecture* (194).[3]

Approximately twenty-five conjectures in twelve pages of text, including three appeals to the argument from silence, results in the following hypothetical conclusion, "The fourth Gospel, *we might say*, was the last plea of first-generation Christianity for a true balance in its devotional and sacramental life . . . "[4] etc., etc., etc. The conclusion leaves little, if any, doubt about the author's antisacramental opinions, but it has not been empirically demonstrated that there is any necessary connection between his opinions and John's theology of the Spirit and baptism.

This is not meant to denigrate the positive role of hypotheses in reconstructing a Johannine theology of the Spirit and baptism. All progress in human knowledge begins with basic assumptions. One does not really think without them. Even so exact a discipline as mathematics has its axioms. Like the axiom, however, the hypothesis must have some measure of self-evident probability to make it credible. Its inner logic must display a consistency and coherence with supporting data. When the supporting data base is itself a series of unsupported conjectures, even consistency and coherence cannot subsititute for probability. Methodologically, the most that can be said then for his conclusion is that it represents conceptualization without exegetical verification.

John 3:5

The most significant exegetical effort to resolve the question posed by John 3:5 (ὕδωρ καὶ πνεῦμα, "water and Spirit") is the following observation:

The phrase is a hendiadys, and the single preposition governing both words indicates that ὕδωρ καὶ πνεῦμα forms a single concept—water-and-Spirit. This implies either that Christian conversion-initiation is a (theological) unity of which both water-baptism and Spirit-baptism are integral parts [in which case the verse does not say how they are related], or that the water is a symbol of the life-giving power of the Spirit as in 4.14 and 7.38.[5]

A preference is expressed for the latter "as more likely" for the following reasons. (1) Water is a symbol in the OT of God's activity "in quickening men to life," and (2) in Jewish thought, it is frequently linked with "the eschatological recreation and renewal effected by the gift of the Spirit."[6] Dunn concludes at this point that "The further we set John's Gospel into the context of Palestinian Judaism, as expressed particularly in the Qumran sect, the more weight we will give to this use of 'water' with Spirit to symbolize renewal by Spirit."[7]

The viability of this conclusion is dependent upon the accuracy of two assumptions: (1) the figure ὕδωρ καὶ πνεῦμα is a hendiadys, and (2) it has been correctly interpreted as "the water-of-the-Spirit [water which stands symbolically for Spirit] . . . which effects birth ἄνωθεν."[8]

Hendiadys is defined as "the expression of an idea by two nouns connected by *and* (as *cups* and *gold*) instead of by a noun and an adjective (as *golden cups*)."[9] A simple test of the hendiadys in each instance is to transpose the figure into the corresponding noun and adjective. It should then yield the same sense in both instances.

Dunn draws a parallel with πνεῦμα καὶ ἀλήθεια, and says, "As it is the Spirit-of-truth (πνεῦμα καὶ ἀλήθεια) who makes spiritual worship possible (4.23f.),[10] so it is the water-of-the-Spirit (ὕδωρ καὶ πνεῦμα) which effects birth ἄνωθεν."[11] When ἀλήθεια is read adjectively, the result is "truthful spirit." Conversely, when πνεῦμα is translated adjectively, the result is "spiritual truth." Neither transposition yields the meaning, "the Spirit-of truth." So far the results are not promising, and one must question whether interpreting these figures of speech as hendiadys really represents John's intention.

On the other hand, pursuing the idea of a hendiadys in 3:5 results in a reversal of the thesis that the water is "a symbol of the life-giving power of the Spirit." When πνεῦμα is transposed into its cognate adjective πνευματικόν—there is no adjectival form for ὕδωρ in NT Greek—the result is *spiritual water*. The hendiadys thus understood places the emphasis on water rather than upon Spirit. The clause would then read, "unless one is born (ἐξ) of/from spiritual water." The preposition ἐκ "is always used with the ablative case," expressing source (origin) or separation.[12] Thus, the unity of the hendiadys results from absorbing Spirit into water, rather than water into Spirit—a complete reversal of Dunn's thesis.

The alternate interpretation of the hendiadys as "water-which-is (also) Spirit,"[13] parallels the interpretation "spiritual water." The logic of the conversion-initiation thesis requires that this interpretation be rejected, as is also the corollary view that "the water is made potent by the Spirit."[14] Nevertheless, both of these interpretations reflect the meaning of a hendiadys correctly, while Dunn's interpretation is incorrect.

In the light of the foregoing discussion, the argument for a hendiadys is not entirely convincing. It is better then to recognize that water and Spirit, while closely coordinated, are not absorbed into each other. The following admonition is apropos, "Exaggerated spiritualism has always been embarrassed by this first term, *water*, and has sought to identify it with the second."[15]

Notes

[1]Dunn, op. cit., pp. 183–194.

[2]Ibid., p. 183.

[3]Italics added; page numbers also follow the citation.

[4]Dunn, op. cit., p. 194.

[5]Ibid., p. 192.

[6]Ibid.

[7]Ibid.

[8]Ibid.

[9]*Webster's Seventh New Collegiate Dictionary* (Springfield, MA: G. & C. Merriam Company [1963]).

[10]The translation is debatable. The RSV translates "spirit and truth"—"spirit" is lower case.

[11]Dunn, op. cit., p. 192.

[12]A. T. Robertson and W. Hersey Davis, *A New Short Grammar of the Greek New Testament* (New York: Harper & Brothers Publishers [1933]), p. 257.

[13]C. H. Dodd, *The Interpretation of the Fourth Gospel*, 312; quoted by Dunn, op. cit., p. 192.

[14]E. K. Lee, *The Religious Thought of St. John*, p. 189; quoted by Dunn, op. cit., p. 192.

[15]F. Godet, *Commentary on the Gospel of St. John*, II, trans. M. D. Cusin and S. Taylor (Edinburgh: T. & T. Clark, 1892), p. 49.

Chapter 15

I John

The chapter, "The Spirit and the Word in the Letters of John,"[1] opens with a hesitant concession to the Pentecostal and sacramental viewpoints:

The author of the Fourth Gospel may have believed that the apostles' Spirit-baptism was distinct from and subsequent to their regeneration, and also that water-baptism played a key part in the birth ἄνωθεν.[2]

Assuming then the Johannine authorship of the epistles that bear his name, it is innocuous to ask, in the light of these concessions, if Pentecostals and sacramentalists "find any further support for their views in his other writings."[3] If John believed in Spirit-baptism subsequent to regeneration and a sacramental efficacy in water baptism, his silence on these points in his epistles would be irrelevant to the discussion. Only if it could be shown that the epistles contradicted the Pentecostal and sacramental interpretations would the conversion-initiation thesis be served.

While the chapter title encompasses the "Letters" of John, only passages from his first epistle are cited.

I John 2:20, 27; 3:9

These three passages are treated together because χρῖσμα, "anointing," and σπέρμα, "seed," are presumed to refer to the same thing, "either the Word or the Spirit, or the Spirit with the Word."[4] It is "usu(ally) taken to mean anointing w(ith) the Holy Spirit."[5] After surveying the suggested range of meaning, Dunn concludes that "the χρῖσμα is the Spirit—albeit the Spirit working in conjunction with, or even through the Word."[6]

The word χρῖσμα in the NT is unique to I John, occurring there three times, 2:20, 27 (twice): "But you have an *anointing* from the Holy One . . . the *anointing* which you received from Him abides in you, and you have no need for anyone to teach you . . . His *anointing* teaches you about all things."[7] It is not possible, therefore, to appeal to parallel NT usages to expand the range of meaning. Several allusions in the context, however, relate it to the Johannine theological ambience, which, in turn, illumines its meaning.

First, the anointing comes from the Holy One (ἀπὸ τοῦ ἁγίου). The phrase echoes John 6:69, ὁ ἅγιος τοῦ θεοῦ "the Holy One of God." Second, the reference to Jesus as the "Paraclete with the Father" (2:1) relates it to the Johannine Paraclete sayings. Third, in I John 2:27, it is the anointing which "teaches" them, so that they are able to distinguish between the deceptions of the antichrists and the truth of Christ.

It was pointed out in the discussion of the Paraclete sayings that one of the *functions* of the ἄλλον παράκλητον, the "other Paraclete" (the Holy Spirit), is to teach. The χρῖσμα of I John 2:20, 27 is also to be understood as a *functional*, and not as an ontological manifestation of the Holy Spirit. To what extent one hears an echo of the cognate verb, χρίω (Acts 10:38), will depend upon his theological orientation. Certainly, the Pentecostal understanding of it as baptism in the Spirit cannot be precluded a priori.

The second word under discussion here, σπέρμα, occurs three times in the Gospel of John in reference to the seed of Abraham or David. It occurs in I John only in 3:9, "No one born of God commits sin: for God's nature (σπέρμα) abides in him." That is to say, σπέρμα equals "the beginning or germ of a new life planted by the Spirit of God."[8] An important fact that emerges from this is that σπέρμαις is used in 3:9 *ontologically,* not functionally.

Thus χρῖσμα and σπέρμα refer to two distinct results of the Holy Spirit's action, the former *functional,* the latter *ontological.* The epistles of John do not refine these actions more specifically in favor of either the Pentecostal or the conversion-initiation theses. For the resolution of the problem, one must look to ancillary sources. It is here that our previous discussion of John 20:22 and John 3:5 tips the scale in favor of the Pentecostal understanding that the anointing here refers to the baptism in the Spirit subsequent to conversion.

The charge of Gnosticism obliquely leveled at Pentecostals[9] is gratuitous. The rationale for this indictment is not, as one might expect, exegetical; it is simply an ad hominem, for, "only they have had this 'second blessing', and all other Christians are less well equipped for service and much poorer in spiritual experience."[10] True, Pentecostals are a minority in the churches, albeit a rapidly growing minority. It is also true that "they believe *all* Christians could and should have this greater and deeper experience of God."[11] In the Pentecostal perspective, this was normative Christian experience in the apostolic Church, that is, if the book of Acts is a credible witness. Hence, John would have no reason to suggest "that the anointing of the Spirit is an experience which some Christians may not possess."[12]

For reasons too complex to discuss here, this ceased to be true relatively early in Church history, but this does not justify a charge of Gnosticism against contemporary Pentecostals who seek to recover (at least for themselves) what was universal and authentic in the experience of the apostolic Church. Does the fault then, if fault there be, lie with the Pentecostals, or with those who would dissolve this distinctive element in NT experience into a unitary conversion-initiation thesis, that by its propositional nature would perpetuate a noncharismatic ethos as normative?

I John 5:6–12

The discussion of I John 5:6–12 opens with a question: "Does John have the Christian sacraments in mind here?"[13] Even a cursory survey of the exegetical literature will reveal the wide diversity of opinion pro and con on the question. While it is admittedly difficult to avoid partisan commitments completely, our response is an effort to interpret the text in a manner consistent with what we perceive to be the intentionality of the context.

The historical background of I John is the Gnostic controversy that threatened the very life of the Church toward the end of the first century. Explicit allusions in I John show that it was Docetic Gnosticism that posed an immediate threat, e.g., "every spirit which confesses that Jesus Christ has come in flesh is of God" (4:2). Those who refused to acknowledge His actual humanity are anathematized as antichrists. I John 5:6–8 is an explicit affirmation of the authenticity of the incarnation, "This is he who came (ἐστιν ὁ ἐλθὼν = His incarnation) by water (John's baptism) and blood (His crucifixion), Jesus Christ, not with water only but with water and blood" (v.6).

Water and blood refer to the events that marked the beginning and the end of Jesus' ministry, namely, his baptism and his crucifixion. A literal interpretation of the blood and water that issued from the side of the crucified One, John 19:34, reflects a similar anti-Docetic polemic. The Living Bible provides an ingenious paraphrase of the passage in these words, "So we have these three witnesses: the voice of the Holy Spirit in our hearts, the voice from heaven at Christ's baptism, and the voice before he died."

While this exegesis parallels in essential details Dunn's interpretation—one of the rare instances in which we have been able to agree—we part company with him in his conclusion that "even if John 3:5 can justly be understood to indicate the important role of waterbaptism in regeneration . . . I John certainly gives the sacramentalist no further scope, since *it does not even mention* the Christian rite."[14] Strange logic indeed that finds the argument from silence its final defense. Granted the silence of I John on the Christian rite of baptism, then it offers "no further scope" to the antisacramentalist's thesis either. While the debate may thus result in *no decision*, so far as I John is concerned, the tentative concession in favor of John 3:5 tips the scale in favor of the sacramentalist's fundamental thesis.

Notes

[1]Dunn, op. cit., pp. 195–204.
[2]Ibid., p. 195.
[3]Ibid.
[4]Ibid.
[5]Bauer, Arndt, Gingrich.
[6]Dunn, op. cit., p. 197. The range of meaning surveyed includes "a sacramental rite either of baptism or anointing . . . the Word, the Gospel . . . the Spirit alone, and even as distinct from conversion-initiation . . . the Spirit as given in baptism, or in some more complex rite" (pp. 195, 196).
[7]NASB, italics added.
[8]Bauer, Arndt, Gingrich.
[9]Dunn, op. cit., p. 199.
[10]Ibid.
[11]Ibid.
[12]Ibid., p. 204.
[13]Ibid., p. 200.
[14]Ibid., p. 204.

Chapter 16

Hebrews

The exposition of the conversion-initiation hypothesis in "The Spirit and Baptism in Hebrews"[1] involves two passages, Heb. 6:1–6 and 10:22.

Heb. 6:1–6

The conclusion of the argument from Heb. 6:1–6 is summarized in the following dictum:

> The close connection of baptism with repentance and faith on the one hand, and with laying on of hands on the other, means that this passage also tells against rather than for the Pentecostals . . . His [the initiate's] repentance and faith came to its vital climax in *this single rite* of baptism-laying on of hands, and to this repentance and faith the Spirit was given."[2]

It remains now to determine whether or not the exegesis of the texts will support this conclusion.

In 6:1f. there are six foundational elements: (1) "repentance from dead works," (2) "faith toward God," (3) "instruction about ablutions" (βαπτισμῶν διδαχῆς), (4) "the laying on of hands," (5) "the resurrection of the dead," and (6) "eternal judgement."

As foundational doctrines, they reflect the instruction given to catechumens. This is supported by the interpretation of τῆς ἀρχῆς τοῦ Χριστοῦ, "the elementary doctrines of Christ," as an objective genitive, i.e., the teachings about Christ whereby the catechumens were prepared for baptism.

Of the six foundational doctrines, numbers three and four—washings/baptisms and laying on of hands—are pivotal for the conversion-initiation thesis. The plural βαπτισμῶν has proven troublesome for exegetes. Why the plural form? Does it refer simply to Jewish ceremonial lustrations? Does it include Christian baptism? The problem is complicated by the fact that βάπτισμα is the usual word for baptism, while βαπτισμός refers to ritual washings such as those practiced by the Jews. However, this is not a conclusive argument against "the reference to Christian baptism in view of the strongly supported reading of βαπτισμῷ, in Col. 2:12."[3]

If one looks further for a reason for the choice of words here, it is implicit in the nature of catechetical instruction. βαπτισμός as the more flexible in its range of meaning could the more readily encompass "teaching about baptisms,"[4] including John's baptism, Jewish ceremonial washings, and Christian baptism. An understanding of each would be important for the preparation of the catechumen.

There seems to be no adequate reason to dispute what amounts to a consensus that the fourth doctrine, the laying on of hands, refers to the impartation of the Holy Spirit, whether as part of a single conversion-initiation rite remains to be decided. The crux of the conversion-initiation thesis centers on the use of the enclitic particle τε in the phrase ἐπιθέσεως τε χειρῶν. It is claimed that "the very unusual use of τε (instead of καί) suggests that what is envisaged is a single ceremony, like that in Acts 19, the single rite of initiation."[5] In other words, the use of τε instead of καί ties baptism and the laying on of hands so closely together that they may be regarded as a single rite.

The argument is flawed, however, by an important textual oversight. While it is true that τε does connect "clauses thereby indicating a close relationship betw(een) them,"[6] this is not sufficient of itself to support the claim of a "single rite of baptism/laying on of hands." Overlooked in Dunn's exegesis here is the strongly attested τε in the next clause ἀναστάσεως (τε) νεκρῶν, "*and* the resurrection of the dead."[7]

In the earlier Nestle-Aland, *Novum Testamentum Graece* text, the τε in this clause was relegated to the textual apparatus as a variant reading. In the more recent Aland, Black, Metzger, Wikgren, *Greek New Testament* (1966), the τε is placed in the text as the preferred reading. The resultant text reads, βαπτισμῶν διδαχῆς, ἐπιθέσεώς τε χειρῶν, ἀναστάσεώς τε νεκρῶν, καὶ κρίματος αἰωνίου, "of instruction about washings, and (τε) laying on of hands, and (τε) the resurrection of the dead, and (καί) eternal judgment."[8] The τε . . . τε . . . καί introduces an ascensive force. Thus instruction about baptism(s) is related equally to the two subsequent clauses, and culminates in "eternal judgment," the theme of the passage for those who apostatize. We conclude, therefore, that in the relation of baptism to the laying on of hands, the use of τε instead of καί *does not validate* the claim of a "single rite of initiation."

While advocacy of the conversion-initiation thesis shifts next to 6:4f., the nature of the argument remains essentially the same. While acknowledging that the relationship of the clauses is uncertain, it is, nonetheless, claimed "that the middle two [clauses] are closely bound together by the τε . . καί,'' which with the repetition of γευσαμένους suggests the following structure:

ἅπαξ φωτισθέντας γευσαμένους τε τῆς δωρεᾶς τῆς ἐπουρανίου
καὶ μετόχους γενηθέντας πνεύματος ἁγίου
καὶ καλὸν γευσαμένους θεοῦ ῥῆμα
δυνάμεις τε μέλλοντος αἰῶνος[9]

who have once been enlightened
and (τε) have tasted of the heavenly gift
and (καί) have been made partakers of the Holy Spirit,
and (καί) have tasted the good word of God
and (τε) the powers of the age to come,''[10]

His analysis of the passage leads Dunn to the following conclusion, ''The once-for-all illumination consisted in, on the one hand, a tasting of the heavenly gift and coming to share in the Holy Spirit, and on the other, a tasting of the word of God and powers of the age to come.''[11] Thus the first and second clauses are joined together serially, as are the third and fourth. All of which are then related to the Spirit, ''which we have seen elsewhere to be the central element in and decisive mark of conversion-initiation.''[12]

It should be observed, however, that in the above structural analysis of the clauses more than a simple τε . . . καί pattern is discernible. The asymmetrical τε . . . καί . . . καί . . . τε suggests by its chiastic structure a more complex literary period which complicates even more the uncertainty of the relationship of the clauses to one another.

Nevertheless, adopting the logic of the argument on the use of τε in 6:1f., it is noteworthy that τε with δωρεᾶς does not join closely this clause with the following one, πνεύματος ἁγίου, as Dunn suggests. Δωρεᾶς and πνεύματος ἁγίου are not joined by τε but by the more general καί. It cannot be argued on this basis then that ''they received the gift which *is* the Spirit himself.''[13]

On the other hand, the τε with δωρεᾶς relates it closely to the preceding φωτισθέντας, while πνεύματος ἁγίου is more loosely coordinated with δωρεᾶς by καί.

If the heavenly gift is not ''the gift which *is* the Spirit himself,'' what can it be? This raises also the question: Who are the enlightened? While the equation φωτισθέντας = βαπτισθέντας is rejected as ''wholly improbable,''[14] the suggestion is not to be rejected magisterially. The aorist participle connotes a specific act in Christian initiation. As a matter of fact, the Syriac text of Heb. 6:4 reads "baptism" (*l^ema'mudi-ta*) for φωτισθέντας, "enlightenment."[15] Furthermore, enlightenment and instruction are frequently used interchangeably. Justic Martyr (A.D. 110–165) called baptism illumination, because the instruction which accompanied it illuminated the mind.[16]

The heavenly gift "may have been the common meal, sometimes called the holy meal . . . to which sectarians were admitted as a final step in initiation."[17] Its extension to the Eucharist is a natural corollary.[18]

While the identification of φωτισθέντας = baptism, and τῆς δωρεᾶς τῆς ἐπουρανίου = Eucharist is in keeping with the sacramental ambience of Hebrews, it cannot be affirmed dogmatically. Nevertheless, the plausibility of the identification reinforces the conclusion that there are no grounds exegetically for the claim of a "single rite of baptism-laying on of hands."

Heb. 10:22

The exhortation "let us draw near" (προσερχώμεθα) is followed by two participial clauses, "with our hearts sprinkled (ῥεραντισμένοι) from an evil conscience and our bodies washed (λελουσμένοι) with pure water." The "sprinkling" and "washing" may echo the injunctions for the preparation of the priests for their duties (Ex. 29:4, et al.).[19] For the Psalmist clean hands and a pure heart were prerequisite for those who would stand in "the holy place" (Psalm 24:4). For the writer of Hebrews, those who would draw near (to the altar) must have their hearts sprinkled (with the blood of Christ, 9:13, 14) and their bodies washed with pure water. The latter parallels Luke's and Paul's emphasis upon baptism as the washing away of sins, which is substantively more than an outward washing of the body.[20] The "imagery is consistent with this sacrificial and liturgical context."[21]

That these reflect "two complementary aspects of Christian conversion-initiation: the outward and the inward—the sprinkling of the heart and the washing of the body,"[22] does not pose a problem in exegesis. However, the extrapolation from this of an "inward, spiritual and outward, material antithesis"[23] is not an exegetical datum. The "sharp contrast" between an outward cleansing of the flesh and an inward cleansing of the conscience in 9:13f. does not support the idea of an antithesis in 10:22. The contrast in 9:13f. is between the old covenant and the new covenant in which "the blood of Christ" supersedes "the blood of goats and bulls."

The whole thesis of Hebrews is the superiority of the new covenant to the old covenant. It is tantamount to a denial of this thesis to say that for the writer of Hebrews, "Christian baptism ranks with and is no different from Jewish βαπτισμοί (9.10) in that its cleansing reaches no further than the body."[24] Wherein then is the superiority of the new covenant over the old covenant?

Christian baptism in its *outward form* may "closely resemble Jewish lustrations" (βαπτισμοί), but the meaning is substantively different. This is all the more apparent, if it be understood that the writer of the Hebrews shared the theological ambience of Paul. In what sense, for example, do Jewish βαπτισμοί constitute the Pauline "washing of regeneration?"[25]

A final summation raises more questions than it answers. It is asserted that the commonly held belief that conversion precedes baptism and that baptism as a confession of a previous commitment cannot be found in the NT. Dunn concludes, therefore, that "Baptism is the act of faith, part of the total cleansing which enables the convert to draw near and to enter the Holy of Holies by the way opened for him by Jesus (vv. 11–22)."[26]

There is an element of ambiguity in this statement. What is the relation of baptism as the act of faith and baptism as a confession of a previous commitment? Is the act of faith itself the act of commitment? Their juxtaposition in the text would support this conclusion. If this is the intention here, then baptism is not *an* act; it is *the* act that constitutes commitment. The logic seems irresistible. No baptism, no commitment. No commitment, no conversion. No conversion, no salvation.

In the light of this conclusion, how is one to understand the experience of Paul and Cornelius? The question is raised in the context of our previous discussion of Acts. Both received the gift of the Holy Spirit *before* they were baptized. Was their commitment made *before* or *after* they received the gift of the Spirit? It is an anomaly, indeed, if their *act of faith* = baptism = commitment followed their reception of the Spirit. One might argue on this basis that faith/baptism/commitment were not essential to receiving the gift of the Spirit.

We conclude, therefore, that the propositional logic of the conversion-initiation thesis is flawed and fails to account for the paradoxes of NT spirituality.

Notes

[1]Dunn, op. cit., pp. 205–214.

[2]Ibid., p. 208, italics added.

[3]Ibid., p. 207.

[4]Bauer, Arndt, Gingrich.

[5]Dunn, op. cit., p. 207.

[6]Bauer, Arndt, Gingrich.

[7]NASB, italics added.

[8]Ibid.

[9]Dunn, op. cit., p. 208.

[10]NASB. The placement of the commas indicates a 3.2 parallelism rather than the 2.2 suggested by Dunn.

[11]Dunn, op. cit., p. 209.

[12]Ibid.

[13]Ibid.

[14]Ibid., p. 210.

[15]George Wesley Buchanan, *To the Hebrews*, Vol. 36, *The Anchor Bible* (Garden City: Doubleday & Company, Inc., 1972), p.106.

[16]Ibid.

[17]Ibid.

[18]*Recognitions of Clement*, Vol. VIII, *The Ante-Nicene Fathers*, eds. Alexander Roberts and James Donaldson, trans. Thomas Smith (Grand Rapids: Wm. B. Eerdmans Publishing Company, 1951), p. 132, n.1.

[19]Marcus Dods, "The Epistle to the Hebrews," Vol. IV, *The Expositor's Greek Testament* (Grand Rapids: Wm. B. Eerdmans Publishing Company, [n.d.]), p. 296.

[20]Acts 2:38; 22:16; I Cor. 6:11; Eph. 5:26.

[21]Buchanan, op. cit., p. 169.

[22]Dunn, op. cit., p. 212.

[23]Ibid.

[24]Ibid., pp. 212, 213.

[25]Titus 3:5; cf. I Cor. 6:11; Eph. 5:26; also John 3:5.

[26]Dunn, op. cit. p. 214.

Chapter 17

I Peter

The development of the theme, "Conversion-Initiation in Peter,"[1] is confined to the first epistle. Four texts are the subject of comment in the following order: I Peter 3:21; 1:2; 1:22; 1:3, 23. The most important of these from the standpoint of the conversion-initiation hypothesis is I Peter 3:21. It is apparently for this reason that it is discussed first.[2]

I Peter 3:21

As Noah and his family were saved through water, so baptism, as the fulfillment of the Noachian type, "now saves you." Noah's deliverance from the flood is a "foreshadowing," or type (τύπος) to which baptism corresponds as the antitype.[3] But how does baptism save? The key phrase is συνειδήσεως ἀγαθῆς ἐπερώτημα. Depending on whether the genitive is regarded as subjective or objective, it may be interpreted as (1)the request addressed to God *by* a clear conscience, or (2) the request addressed to God *for* a clear conscience. The evidence of the versions is divided, as Dunn indicates, between either "a pledge proceeding from or to maintain a clear conscience or attitude (JB, TEV)," or "an appeal or prayer to God for a clear conscience (RSV, NEB)."[4]

The Greek phrase is indeed "puzzling," and "our inability to catch its precise meaning is frustrating."[5] However, the ambiguity need not be a total impasse. The baptismal context lends credibility to the suggestion that "ἐπερώτημα may even indicate a specific moment in the ritual of initiation—the act of confession or moment of (silent) prayer immediately prior to the immersion."[6] There is, in fact, textual support for it in the Peshitta *mawdeyn*, "confessing," i.e., "God with a clean conscience."[7]

The conclusion that follows is acceptable, as far as it goes, "What Peter was saying is quite unambiguous at this point: baptism saves, not in its washing away the filth of the flesh, but by expressing man's repentance and/or faith to God."[8] The incompleteness of this conclusion results from its failure to recognize the full significance of the instrumental δι' ἀναστάσεως Ἰησοῦ Χριστοῦ. Neither the water rite nor the confession is an end in itself. They are efficacious because of the resurrection of Jesus. The NIV captures the nuance correctly, "it [baptism] saves you by the resurrection of Jesus Christ."

Thus the salvific effect of baptism involves more then the baptismal confession of faith. It is through the resurrection that God's saving power is extended to mankind. The convert's baptismal confession is rendered efficacious through (διά) the resurrection of Jesus Christ "into whose death and resurrection we were baptized."[9] Baptism is, therefore, more than an expression of "man's repentance and/or faith to God." It is an identification with Jesus in His death and resurrection. It is not accurate to say, then, "that baptism is the means by which men come to God rather than that by which God comes to men."[10] Paradoxical though it may seem, both statements are true.

Baptized into Christ's death, we rise to walk in newness of life, that is to say, His resurrection life (Rom. 6:3f.). "I have been crucified with Christ; it is no longer I who live, but Christ who lives in me" (Gal. 2:20) is simply another way of describing this baptismal union. These are the words of the seer, the mystic, the man "caught up into Paradise" (II Cor. 12:4); they are not the propositional logic of the dogmatician.

It may be objected that this makes Paul's doctrine of baptism normative for Peter. The objection is not a serious obstacle to this interpretation, because of the Pauline influences discernible in I Peter. "That the epistle is intimately related to the Pauline theology and message" is, in the opinion of Bo Reicke, "inescapable."[11] It cannot be conceded, therefore, "that I Peter 3:21 is the nearest approach to a definition of baptism that the NT affords."[12] Peter does not have the final, nor even the definitive word on baptism.

I Peter 1:2

The key words are κατὰ πρόγνωσιν θεοῦ πατρός, "according to the predestination of God the Father."[13] The subject is God's election. Within this context, ὑπακοήν, "obedience," and ῥαντισμόν, "sprinkling," (with the blood of Christ), are too general in their reference to provide evidence for the conversion-initiation thesis. Since repentance, faith, baptism, and the gift of the Spirit are not mentioned, only a speculative reconstruction can discern indistinct echoes of a conversion-initiation paradigm.

I Peter 1:22

A brief comment will suffice here. The reader is informed that "Once again the cleansing is moral and spiritual (τὰς ψυχὰς ὑμῶν ἡγνικότες, [having purified your souls]), as also in James 4:8 and I John 3:3, and *there is no reference to baptism.*"[14] Three sentences later the reader is again informed that "In I Peter this probably refers to the once-for-all obedience at conversion-initiation (ἡγνικότες—perfect); in fact *it may well refer to baptism.*"[15] We have no suggestions for resolving the apparent contradiction.

I Peter 1:3, 23

Although "there is no thought of baptism"[16] here, it is, nonetheless, concluded that "We are once again within that complex event conversion-initiation whose unity cannot be broken."[17] Since "there is no thought of baptism" here, the conversion-initiation thesis lacks a critical component. Its only support comes from an arbitrary paradigm of conversion-initiation contexts "whose unity cannot be broken." The Pentecostal would respond that this unity has yet to be demonstrated.

All that can be documented from these texts is that believers are born again. Once again, the conversion-initiation thesis lacks empirical and incontrovertible evidence. As this critique has repeatedly stressed, none of the data offered in support of the conversion-initiation thesis, as defined by Professor Dunn, can be regarded as convincing, much less conclusive.

As one would anticipate, the chapter closes on an anti-Pentecostal note. It is introduced by a rhetorical question, "What of the Spirit and the relevance of I Peter to Pentecostal doctrine?"[18] Although there is not a single unambiguous reference to Pentecost in I Peter, it is, nonetheless, suggested that "1.12 may be an allusion to Pentecost (ἀποσταλέντι ἀπ' οὐρανοῦ)."[19] The general reference here to "the Holy Spirit sent from heaven" is extrapolated into the following categorical conclusion, "At all events we can say firmly that the Pentecostal doctrine of the baptism in the Spirit has no foothold in I Peter, and that on the contrary, I Peter is sufficiently close to Paul on this point to confirm our complete rejection of this doctrine."[20]

It is ironic, but nonetheless characteristic of the methodology of *Baptism in the Holy Spirit*, that the final rejection of Pentecostal doctrine (and experience!) is not adduced from Peter's words but deduced from Peter's silence.

Notes

[1]Dunn, op. cit., pp. 215–223.

[2]Ibid., pp. 215–219.

[3]Bauer, Arndt, Gingrich.

[4]Dunn, op. cit., p. 217.

[5]Ibid.

[6]Ibid.

[7]*The Holy Bible Translated from Ancient Eastern Manuscripts*, trans. George M. Lamsa (Philadelphia: A. J. Holman Company, 1961).

[8]Dunn, op. cit., 218.

[9]Henry Alford, *The Greek Testament*, IV (Cambridge: Deighton, Bell, and Co., 1866), p. 368.

[10]Dunn, op. cit., p. 219.

[11]Bo Reicke, *The Epistles of James, Peter, and Jude*, Vol. 37, *The Anchor Bible* (Garden City: Doubleday & Company, Inc., [1964]), p. 70.

[12]Dunn, op. cit., p. 219.

[13]Bauer, Arndt, Gingrich.

[14]Dunn, op. cit., p. 220; italics added.

[15]Ibid.; italics added.

[16]Ibid., p. 221.

[17]Ibid.

[18]Ibid.

[19]Ibid., p. 222.

[20]Ibid.

Conclusion

A lengthy and detailed argument can precipitate a like response, but we have attempted to minimize the tediousness of this kind of answer. In order to assist further the reader, we have summarized briefly the discussion in the following points.

1. John the Baptist's baptism in the Spirit and fire belongs to the fulfillment of OT prophetic eschatology. The Pentecostal baptism in the Spirit for power in mission belongs to NT apocalyptic eschatology. Dunn's failure to distinguish these respective eschatological frames of reference exacerbates the confusion between Jordan and Pentecost in the conversion-initiation hypothesis.

2. The assumption that Jesus' baptism in the Spirit at Jordan was primarily initiatory—it supposedly inaugurated the new age and covenant—is simply a theological construct at variance with the available exegetical data. Jesus' Spirit-baptism is identified textually with empowerment for mission. It requires considerable theological ingenuity to read conversion-initiation into Jesus' experience with the Spirit at Jordan. However, were the theme of power-in-service removed from Luke/Acts, Luke's pneumatology would be unintelligible.

3. Jesus did not enter the new age and covenant through His baptism in the Spirit at Jordan. Jordan belongs to the dénouement of prophetic eschatology. The presumed parallelism between His experience at Jordan and the disciples' experience at Pentecost does not validate the claim that it was the Pentecostal baptism in the Spirit that ushered His disciples into the new age and covenant. That a parallelism between Jordan and Pentecost does exist is not denied. The common denominator between them, however, is empowerment for service within their respective eschatological frames of reference.

4. The contention that the Samaritans were not yet Christians, even though they believed and were baptized, fails of any serious exegetical proof. The effort to validate it exegetically by the use of the verb πιστεύειν with a dative object cannot bear the burden of proof Dunn places upon it.

5. Although Paul's instantaneous conversion on the Damascus road was "sharply questioned," the denial of this view lacks cogency. An examination of the title "Lord" on Paul's lips, and Ananias's greeting, "Brother," argues for the conclusion that Paul was converted in his Damascus encounter with the glorified Jesus.

6. The interpretive norm for the experience of Cornelius and his household is supplied by Acts 11:17. He and his household received the same gift of the Spirit as the apostles at Pentecost. Thus, one's interpretation of Pentecost predetermines one's understanding of Cornelius's experience. Consequently, as the baptism in the Spirit of the Church on the day of Pentecost was empowerment for work and worship; so also was it in the experience of the Roman centurion.

7. The exclusion of the Ephesian disciples of John (Acts 19:1–7) from the Christian community in Ephesus rests upon a methodological fallacy. The use of the indefinite pronoun τινες, rather than the definite article οἱ with the noun μαθηταί is not a valid criterion for determining the identity of the Ephesian disciples. The obvious implication of the context is that these were disciples of John the Baptist. They had experienced only John's baptism of repentance. Their subsequent baptism in the name of the Lord Jesus constituted Christian initiation. Their reception of the Holy Spirit through the laying on of Paul's hands was for power in word, worship, and work, a fact evidenced by the charisms of tongues and prophecy.

8. The appeal to Acts 2:38 as "the only verse in Acts that directly relates the three most important elements in conversion-initiation" implies a theological reductionism of the Johannine theology of regeneration with the Lukan theology of power. It is a serious categorical mistake to read conversion-initiation, with its concomitant Johannine doctrine of the new birth, into Luke's gift of the Holy Spirit for power-in-mission.

9. The charge that the Pentecostal position is built "foursquare" on Acts, without support from the Pauline letters, does not prejudice the Pentecostal exegesis. Paul does not distinguish explicitly between the Spirit's actions in conversion and baptism, with the possible exception of I Cor. 12:12f. However, both motifs appear in his epistles.

In Dunn's subsequent debate with sacramentalists, the exegesis of distinctive baptismal contexts is misleading. Instead, the conversion-initiation thesis is defended by an appeal to what Dunn calls "conversion initiation contexts" without regard for "whatever elements are present or absent." However, such a methodology may be dismissed as simply special pleading.

His anti-sacramentalism proceeds, not from an exegesis of the text, but from implicit philosophical/theological a prioris. The polarity between these assumptions and the exegetical evidence emerges as an irreconcilable dichotomy in the assertions that (1) "God operates 'through' and by means of baptism to effect the spiritual transformation," but on the other hand (2), "Baptism does not effect these."

10. In his discussion of John 20:22, Dunn's concession that "the Pentecostal thesis at this point cannot be entirely rejected" irremediably undermines his whole conversion-initiation hypothesis. The subsequent appeal to its unique and unrepeatable dispensational character is a counsel of confusion. It does nothing to rehabilitate the conversion-initiation hypothesis.

11. The discussion of "The Spirit and Baptism in John's Gospel" reveals clearly the conjectural methodology of the conversion-initiation thesis. Twenty-five conjectures in twelve pages of text, including three appeals to the argument from silence, result in a wholly hypothetical conclusion: "The fourth Gospel, we might say, was the last appeal of first-generation Christianity for a true balance in its devotional and sacramental life."

12. The conjectural nature of the conversion-initiation hypothesis is readily apparent in the effort to find conversion-initiation texts/contexts in the epistles. With one possible exception[1] no empirical evidence is offered. The evidence offered in support of the theory is essentially conjecture buttressed by the argument from silence. We must conclude, therefore, that the conversion-initiation hypothesis rests upon *no* empirically verifiable base.

Note

[1]For the text in question refer to our discussion of I Cor. 12:13. The bearing of this passage on the conversion-initiation hypothesis is semantic rather than substantive.

SUBJECT INDEX

INDEX OF SCRIPTURE
REFERENCES